Access to History

General Editor: Keith Randel

France: Renaissance, Religion and Recovery, 1494–1610

Martyn Rady

Hodder & Stoughton

A MEMBER OF THE HODDER HEADLINE GROUP

The cover illustration shows a portrait of Catherine de Medici attributed to Francis Clouet in the Musee de la Ville de Paris, Musee Carnavalet. Courtesy Lauros-Giraudon.

Some other titles in the series:

Luther and the German Reformation 1517–55
Keith Randell   ISBN 0 340 51808 1

John Calvin and the Later Reformation
Keith Randell   ISBN 0 340 52940 7

The Catholic and Counter Reformations
Keith Randell   ISBN 0 340 53495 8

From Revolt to Independence: The Netherlands 1550–1650
Martyn Rady   ISBN 0 340 51803 0

Spain: Rise and Decline 1474–1643
Jill Kilsby   ISBN 0 340 51807 3

The Tsars, Russia Poland and the Ukraine 1462–1725
Martyn Rady   ISBN 0 340 53258 0

Order queries: Please contact Bookpoint Ltd, 39 Milton Park, Abingdon, Oxon OX14 4TD. Telephone: (44) 01235 400414. Fax: (44) 01235 400454. Lines are open from 9 am - 6 pm Monday to Saturday, with a 24-hour message answering service. Email address: orders@bookpoint.co.uk

British Library Cataloguing in Publication Data

Rady, Martyn C.
    France: renaissance, religion and
    Recovery, 1494–1610.—(Access to
    history).
    1.   France. History
    2.   I. Title. II. Series
    944

ISBN 0 340 51804 9

First published in the Access to A-level History series 1988, two impressions
This edited first published 1991
Impression number   12 11   10   9   8   7   6
Year   2004 2003 2002 2001 2000 1999 1998

Copyright © 1988 Martyn Rady

Printed in Great Britain for Hodder & Stoughton Educational, a division of Hodder Headline Plc, 338, Euston Road, London NW1 3BH by Redwood Books, Trowbridge, Wiltshire.

Contents

Preface

To the general reader

Although the *Access to History* series has been designed with the needs of students studying the subject at higher examination levels very much in mind, it also has a great deal to offer the general reader. The main body of the text (i.e. ignoring the Study Guides at the ends of chapters) forms a readable and yet stimulating survey of a coherent topic as studied by historians. However, each author's aim has not merely been to provide a clear explanation of what happened in the past (to interest and inform): it has also been assumed that most readers wish to be stimulated into thinking further about the topic and to form opinions of their own about the significance of the events that are described and discussed (to be challenged). Thus, although no prior knowledge of the topic is expected on the reader's part, she or he is treated as an intelligent and thinking person throughout. The author tends to share ideas and possibilities with the reader, rather than passing on numbers of so-called 'historical truths'.

To the student reader

There are many ways in which the series can be used by students studying History at a higher level. It will, therefore, be worthwhile thinking about your own study strategy before you start your work on this book. Obviously, your strategy will vary depending on the aim you have in mind, and the time for study that is available to you.

If, for example, you want to acquire a general overview of the topic in the shortest possible time, the following approach will probably be the most effective:

1 Read Chapter 1 and think about its contents.
2 Read the 'Making notes' section at the end of Chapter 2 and decide whether it is necessary for you to read this chapter.
3 If it is, read the chapter, stopping at each heading or * to note down the main points that have been made.
4 Repeat stage 2 (and stage 3 where appropriate) for all the other chapters.

If, however, your aim is to gain a thorough grasp of the topic, taking however much time is necessary to do so, you may benefit from carrying out the same procedure with each chapter, as follows:

1 Read the chapter as fast as you can, and preferably at one sitting.
2 Study the flow diagram at the end of the chapter, ensuring that you understand the general 'shape' of what you have just read.

3   Read the 'Making notes' section (and the 'Answering essay questions' section, if there is one) and decide what further work you need to
do on the chapter. In particularly important sections of the book, this
will involve reading the chapter a second time and stopping at each
heading and * to think about (and to write a summary of) what you
have just read.
4   Attempt the 'Source-based questions' section. It will sometimes be
sufficient to think through your answers, but additional understanding
will often be gained by forcing yourself to write them down.

When you have finished the main chapters of the book, study the
'Further Reading' section and decide what additional reading (if any)
you will do on the topic.

   This book has been designed to help make your studies both
enjoyable and successful. If you can think of ways in which this could
have been done more effectively, please write to tell me. In the
meantime, I hope that you will gain greatly from your study of History.

Keith Randell

CHAPTER 1

Background

The kingdom of France at the close of the fifteenth century occupied much the same surface area as modern France. Like today, the country was bounded by the English Channel, the Atlantic and the Mediterranean, while the border with Spain ran along the Pyrenees. The administrative centre of France was Paris, and among the kingdom's most important cities may be counted, then as now, Bordeaux, Toulouse, Lyons, Rouen and Dijon. Nevertheless, there are important differences between the boundaries of modern France and those of 1500. Artois and Cambrai, to the north of Paris, were held by the Habsburg rulers of the Netherlands. Further east, the frontier dissolved into a mosaic of dukedoms and lordships, some of which owed their allegiance to the King of France, others to the Holy Roman Emperor. In the south, the status of Dauphiné and Provence remained uncertain. Neither were regarded as proper parts of France, but instead as territories which belonged personally to the King. Along the southern boundary with Spain, Roussillon was held by the King of Aragon, and Navarre was a small kingdom with its own independent ruler. The cities of Calais and Nice similarly lay outside the French frontier. Calais belonged to the King of England, and Nice to the Duke of Savoy (see map, page 4).

The system of feudal lordship further complicates any attempt to establish the kingdom's frontiers precisely. The Dukes of Lorraine and Montmorency owed their primary allegiance to the King of France, yet both held extensive properties in Germany and the Netherlands. Brittany was considered a part of France, yet since its lord did not pay homage to anyone, it might be viewed as an independent state. Contrastingly, the King of Navarre had substantial estates in France, for which he did homage to the French sovereign. A two-dimensional map is, therefore, an inadequate guide to French national boundaries around 1500. The relationship of the parts to the whole depended upon a complex web of personal allegiances which a map can scarcely reveal.

Altogether the kingdom of France had in 1500 about 15 million inhabitants. These, however, did not make up a homogeneous group. Most Frenchmen identified themselves with the small region in which they lived, and saw themselves as being for instance Burgundians or Normans first and foremost. Linguistic diversity exaggerated local differences. In the south, a language was spoken (the *langue d'oc*) which was more akin to Italian than to French, and in Brittany a Celtic tongue similar to Welsh predominated. Although the spread of modern French, which derives from the *Langue d'oïl* dialect spoken in the north of the country, was proceeding apace, many Frenchmen still found

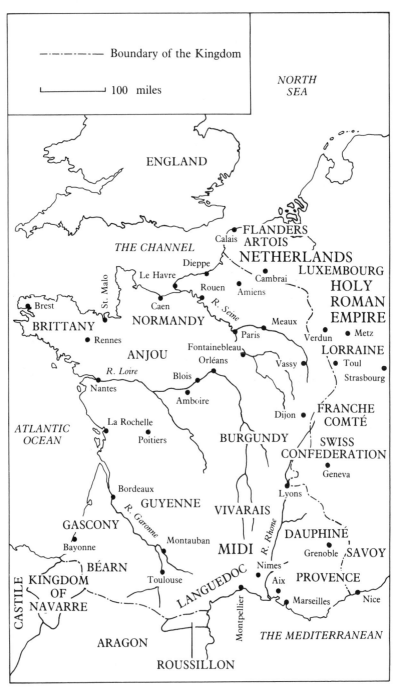

France in 1500

each other incomprehensible. Law added to the problem of language. In most of France, the laws were based on customs which differed from place to place. Only in the south was the law at all codified and even here strong regional differences persisted.

Contemporary French writers based their analysis of social structure on the three 'estates' of the realm: the clergy, the nobility and the 'third estate' (namely, all those who did not belong in the first two categories). This tidy scheme, however, conceals the tremendous variations. The clergy consisted of all churchmen, from the mighty archbishops, who often held extensive properties, down to the poor parish priests. At the top of the noble estate were the *enfants de France*, the King's sons and grandsons. Next to these in importance were the 'princes of the blood', the collateral relatives of the King who belonged to the Bourbon family (see Family Tree, p. 6). Below the princes of the blood stretched a hierarchy of noble ranks, from great lords to humble esquires. Most of these had inherited their titles or earned them in battle. However, during the fifteenth and sixteenth centuries an increasingly large number of noblemen either bought their titles or were awarded them by the King on account of their administrative involvement in the royal service. These newcomers were regularly known as the *noblesse de la robe*, after the cloak of office which they wore, and are as such distinguished from the older *noblesse de l'épée*, whose principal function was to fight for the King. However, since many 'sword-nobles' also performed administrative services for the crown, the distinction between *noblesse de la robe* and *noblesse de l'épée* was often blurred. Like the 'nobles of the sword', many 'robe-nobles' were able to pass on their titles and status to their children. The hereditary character of noble rank did much to conceal the humble origins of many titled families.

Strong rivalries existed among the nobles. The old nobility of the sword resented the newcomers who had bought their titles, and believed them to have debased the whole institution of nobility. Higher up the social scale the great nobles or aristocrats constantly vied with one another for access to the King and for a place in the royal council, wherein the most important matters of state were discussed. On their private lands, many nobles held their own seigneurial or manor courts, which had jurisdiction over their tenants. These seigneurial courts often came into conflict both with one another and with the basic units of royal administration, the bailiwicks and seneschalcies. The squabbles of the nobles and the persistent rivalry of their spokesmen proved to be a major cause of political instability throughout the sixteenth century.

The first and second estates made up only a few per cent of the population of France. Most people belonged to the Third Estate, a wide category which embraced *bourgeoisie* (townsfolk), *roturiers* (freemen) and the few remaining serfs. The third estate bore the brunt of taxation, since unlike the clergy and nobility they did not have exemption from the heavy tax known as the *taille* (which was a tax on people in the north

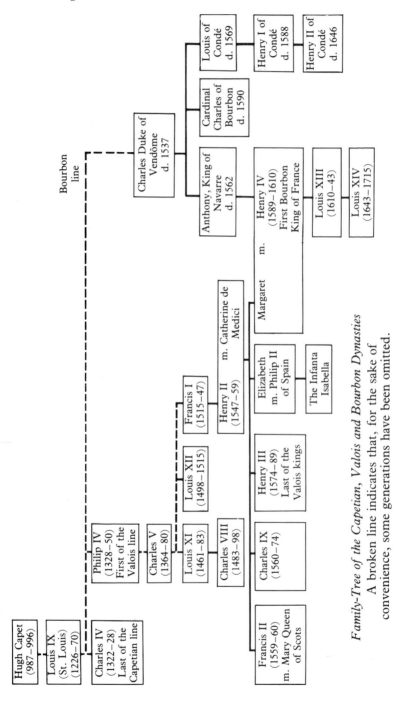

Family-Tree of the Capetian, Valois and Bourbon Dynasties
A broken line indicates that, for the sake of
convenience, some generations have been omitted.

of France, and a tax on land in the south). Nevertheless, except in a few places, the condition of the third estate was steadily improving. Manufacturing and the distributive trades were growing in the towns, and by 1500 the peasantry had reached a new level of prosperity. The more successful members of the third estate were often able to acquire noble status and so enter the ranks of the *noblesse de la robe*. Noble rank conferred many advantages, not just in terms of exemption from the *taille*. Throughout the medieval and early modern period, nobility gave prestige and status. With their coats-of-arms and proud titles, former merchants and wealthy peasants believed themselves to have shrugged off their humble past and to have acquired social respectability.

Ever since the tenth century, the monarchy had been gradually expanding its territories. When the first king of France, Hugh Capet, had taken the throne in 987, he had possessed only a few properties around Paris. Gradually, he and his successors had extended the boundary of their kingdom. By the time Hugh Capet's line expired in the early fourteenth century, the royal territories accounted for much of present-day France. However, the Hundred Years War (1337–1453) fought between the Plantagenet kings of England and the Valois successors to the Capetians upset the process of territorial consolidation. During this period many of the regions which had previously been brought under the crown's authority were able to reacquire their independence.

Following the Hundred Years War, the Valois kings of France gradually reasserted their control over all parts of France. Dauphiné was reacquired in 1456, Burgundy in 1477, Anjou and Provence in 1481, Guyenne in 1491, and Brittany in 1532. All these regions, with the partial exceptions of Dauphiné and Burgundy, were gained peacefully by treaty. Partly as a consequence of these negotiated settlements, the Kings of France were prevented from erasing the traditional institutions of local government and justice which had developed in these areas. In Burgundy, Dauphiné, Provence, Languedoc, Normandy and Guyenne, regional parliaments continued to meet. These provincial estates, as they were known, had the right to negotiate with the King concerning their tax payments and the royal remedy of abuses. Similarly, on the periphery of the kingdom, a number of semi-independent lawcourts or *parlements* functioned. The King was obliged to have his decrees confirmed or 'registered' by the *parlements* of Rouen, Rennes, Bordeaux, Toulouse, Grenoble, Aix-en-Provence and Dijon, before they could be enforced in the regions administered by these bodies. Even within the central portion of the French kingdom, the monarch had to negotiate with the *parlement* of Paris. If the Paris *parlement* refused to register a royal edict, it was considered invalid. The only recourse available to the King was to attend the *parlement* in person, and in the process known as the *lit de justice* actually register the edict himself: a time-consuming and embittering expedient. The principal towns and cities of France also possessed extensive powers of local government. They had their own judicial courts and, like the provincial estates, many claimed to be able to negotiate how much tax they should pay the King.

The absence of an effective parliament embracing the whole of France exaggerated regionalist trends. From the early thirteenth century, an Estates-General, consisting of representatives drawn from the three estates in all of France, had been summoned. But over the next two centuries, this body had shown itself incapable of doing much other than complain. Accordingly, the French kings largely chose not to convene it. Only in times of extreme need – 1484, 1560, 1576 and 1588 – was it called to meet. On all these occasions, the assembled representatives failed to impart any measure of sensible advice. The Estates-General did not meet between 1614 and 1789. In itself this is a telling comment on its political uselessness.

The fragmented character of French government contrasts markedly with the extraordinary authority that was developing in the French monarchy. During the middle ages, the French constitution had been overwhelmingly feudal in content. Relationships had been conceived in contractual terms: the King provided justice, and as a result his subjects gave him their allegiance. If the King acted unfairly, then he need not be obeyed. This concept lingered on into the sixteenth century. In 1523, the French commander and prince of the blood, the Constable Bourbon, rebelled against Francis I on the grounds that the King had treated him unjustly. However, during the late middle ages, feudal notions of loyalty were gradually replaced by more 'absolutist' ones. As a result of the growing influence of Roman Law (legal codes deriving from the time of the late Roman Empire), the idea began to take root that the King was owed an unconditional allegiance by his subjects. Although the King was still bound to follow the laws of God and to abide by the ancient traditions of the realm, it was not for his subjects to decide the limits of his authority. Their obedience was due at all times. As one contemporary commentator observed, whereas in England political authority was jointly vested in King and parliament, in France authority belonged to the King alone. Thus, while England was blessed with a mixed constitution (*dominium politicum et regale*), France laboured under a royal dictatorship (*dominium regale*).

Practice followed theory. In a striking example, in 1544 Francis I sacked the French village of Lagny on account of the rebelliousness of its inhabitants. Thereafter, the King issued warrants forbidding the villagers from seeking recourse in law against the severity of his judgement. Such suspension of the law was almost unknown in England. The last occasion on which it had happened had been in the eleventh century, when William the Conqueror had 'harried' the north.

Even the Tudors covered their despotism with the figleaf of judicial process. Yet, such was the authority belonging to the King of France that he enjoyed the right to suspend the law at will.

The most compelling restraint on all European monarchs was their purse-strings. Although most rulers had a source of ordinary revenue, this was seldom sufficient for their needs. Thus, parliaments had to be called to vote additional or extraordinary money. In return for this grant, the monarch was normally obliged to listen to and to remedy his subjects' grievances. However, during the fifteenth century, the kings of France were able to use the war with England as an excuse for converting extraordinary taxes into ordinary ones. In particular, the salt tax, known as the *gabelle*, and the *taille*, paid by the third estate, ceased to be dependent on a vote of the Estates-General and became permanent taxes. Only in those parts of the kingdom where provincial estates functioned, did the King have to negotiate with his subjects over taxation. Everywhere else, royal officials (*élus*) were in charge of assessment and collection, operating on royal instruction.

A further remarkable feature of the French kingdom was the number of officers in the employ of the crown. By the early sixteenth century, there were perhaps as many as 8000 officials working for the government, either in the judiciary or in the financial organisation. A century later the number had grown to 40 000. Certainly, many of these officers held sinecure posts (*i.e.* posts which carried no actual responsibility). Nevertheless, the growing number of public servants aided the diffusion of royal authority and extended the tentacles of government deep into the countryside. For its population, France had ten times as many royal officers as did England, making it the most heavily 'governed' state in Europe.

Developments in sixteenth-century France are best viewed in the light of trends already evident in the preceding century. First, there was the tremendous authority belonging to the crown. As the theoretical power of the monarchy became steadily transformed into political realities, a reaction occurred amongst those most threatened by the upsurge in royal authority. Thus during the first half of the century, the power of centralised government grew; in the second half, a backlash was experienced in the form of a prolonged period of civil war. Only after more than thirty years of conflict was the earlier trend resumed under the leadership of Henry IV. Secondly, there was the expansionist policy of the crown. Throughout the middle ages, the French monarchy had been extending its territory. Yet, with the borders of the realm so fluid and imprecise, there was no obvious point at which to conclude this process. Certainly, and as we shall see, the wars fought in Italy after 1494 may be explained very much in terms of a desire on the part of the kings of France for prestige and booty. In many respects, however, the involvement of Charles VIII and his successors in the Italian peninsula may be seen as the logical extension of the process of territorial aggrandisement set in train by Hugh Capet in 987.

Making Notes on 'Background'

This chapter introduces sixteenth-century French history by reference both to trends apparent in the middle ages and to developments which occur later on in the century. In reading the chapter you should concentrate on *understanding* what is being said rather than on *making notes* in précis form.

However, a number of terms are given here which will be often repeated in the chapters which follow. Make sure, therefore, that you know what is meant by: 'the estates', 'princes of the blood', *noblesse de la robe*, *noblesse de l'épée*, *bourgeoisie*, 'provincial estates', *parlements*, 'Estates-General', *taille*, and *gabelle*. It would serve you well at this stage to compose your own brief glossary of terms to which you can refer back later.

CHAPTER 2

The Italian and Habsburg–Valois Wars

1 Origins

In 1494 King Charles VIII of France led his armies across the Alps and invaded the Italian peninsula. This event is often regarded as marking the end of the middle ages and the dawn of modern history. In the circumstances attending the invasion, some historians have detected the first examples both of nationalist aggression and of an international Balance of Power. Assuming the same 'bird's eye' view of the past, other historians have considered Charles VIII's attack to be the prelude to 200 years or more of rivalry between France and the Habsburg family, rulers of Spain, the Netherlands and much of central Europe. For Italian writers, the French incursion heralds the beginning of the peninsula's servitude under foreign domination and is, therefore, a major turning-point in their country's history.

With the benefit of hindsight, a case can indeed be made for the French invasion of Italy being a decisive moment in European history. Needless to say, this could not have been known at the time and can have played no part in the reckoning of Charles VIII. Charles's express aim in invading the peninsula was essentially a dynastic or family one. He had inherited a right to part of Italy, the kingdom of Naples, and was bound by honour to pursue his claim. According to Philip of Commynes, one of Charles's advisers:

1 Some lawyers arrived from Provence and advanced certain wills
   of King Charles I, brother of St Louis [King of France 1226–70]
   and of other kings [of Naples] who were from the house of
   France, and other reasons, claiming that not only did the county
5 of Provence belong to the King, but also the kingdom of Naples.

Nevertheless, lawyers' arguments will not entirely explain Charles's decision to invade Italy. In the diplomatic negotiations which preceded the campaign, Charles was ready to surrender his territorial claims to Roussillon, Artois and Franche-Comté in order to win the neutrality of his neighbours, Ferdinand of Aragon and the Emperor Maximilian. To understand fully the reason for Charles's invasion of Italy, we must examine the internal condition of the peninsula and the particular attractions it offered the French King.

* Until the nineteenth century, Italy existed only as a 'geographical expression'. The peninsula was politically divided and had been ever since the sixth century (see map, page 12). By the 1490s, six distinct

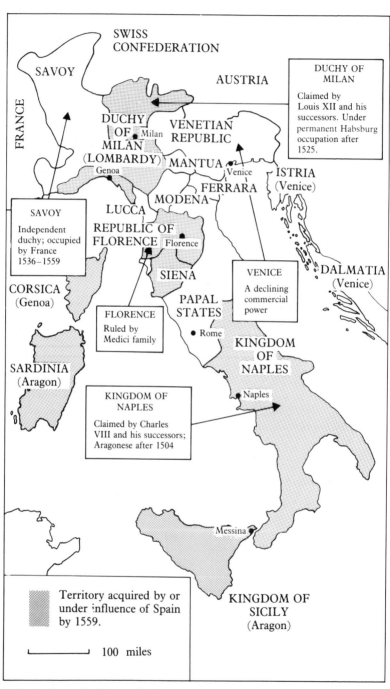

SWISS
CONFEDERATION

SAVOY

FRANCE

AUSTRIA

DUCHY OF
MILAN

Claimed by
Louis XII and his
successors. Under
permanent Habsburg
occupation after
1525.

DUCHY
OF
MILAN
(LOMBARDY)

Milan

VENETIAN
REPUBLIC

MANTUA

Genoa

Venice

ISTRIA
(Venice)

FERRARA

MODENA

LUCCA

SAVOY

Independent
duchy; occupied
by France
1536–1559

REPUBLIC OF
FLORENCE

Florence

CORSICA
(Genoa)

SIENA

VENICE

A declining
commercial
power

DALMATIA
(Venice)

PAPAL
STATES

FLORENCE

Ruled by
Medici family

Rome

SARDINIA
(Aragon)

KINGDOM
OF
NAPLES

KINGDOM OF
NAPLES

Claimed by Charles
VIII and his successors;
Aragonese after 1504

Naples

Messina

Territory acquired by or
under influence of Spain
by 1559.

100 miles

KINGDOM OF
SICILY
(Aragon)

Italy in the early Sixteenth Century

power-blocs were in existence: Rome and the papal states which cut through the middle of the peninsula and lay under the rule of the Pope; the republic of Venice which extended from the eastern Alps to the shores of the Adriatic; the duchy of Milan which occupied the central portion of the plain of Lombardy in the north; the republic of Florence, dominated by the Medici family; and in the south the two kingdoms of Naples and Sicily, which were then ruled by rival branches of the royal house of Aragon. Squeezed between these six states were a number of smaller principalities and territories, most notably the cities of Genoa, Ferrara, Mantua and Siena. Bordering France and straddling the Alps lay the duchy of Savoy, an independent state which functioned very much as a buffer to French expansion.

★ The political fragmentation of Italy had led to prolonged conflict throughout the middle ages. Although in 1454 the warring parties agreed to abandon their squabbles, the peace they devised did not endure. In 1478 Florence made war on the Pope; four years later Venice fought Milan and Naples for possession of Ferrara. No sooner was this conflict resolved than a violent succession dispute arose in the duchy of Milan when the regent, Lodovico Sforza, refused to yield power to his young nephew once he had come of age. The boy, Gian Galeazzo, had married Princess Isabella of Naples and called for support from his father-in-law, King Ferrante I of Naples. In order to win help against Ferrante, Lodovico Sforza looked for allies of his own and eventually requested the aid of Charles VIII of France. In this way, political turmoil within Italy opened the way to French intervention. As a Florentine ambassador was later to explain:

1 Don't let anyone think that if we have many times seen Italy a
  prey for the powers beyond the mountains, this has been caused
  by any other power than by the Italians themselves who have
  turned on each other . . . One can state categorically that the
5 discord of the people of Italy has been that which repressed her,
  weakened her and finally to a large extent placed her under the
  yoke of barbarian servitude.

★ The opportunity given to Charles of making good his claims in Italy at the invitation of one of Italy's most powerful rulers was only matched by the attraction of the peninsula's extraordinary wealth. The Italian cities had long been the most advanced and prosperous centres of trade and manufacturing in the whole of Europe. Although soon to be eclipsed by the new commercial power of Spain and the Netherlands, cities like Milan, Florence and Venice still possessed formidable industrial, financial and mercantile resources. The huge sums gathered in taxes by the rulers of the cities were ostentatiously displayed in magnificent buildings and in artistic patronage. Thus the reputation of the peninsula grew as a land of plenty. Commynes, on visiting the duchy of Milan, could not disguise his admiration: 'I have never seen a more beautiful piece of land nor a more valuable one . . . The duke raises 650 000 to 700 000 ducats a year.' Arriving in Venice on a diplomatic mission, he was similarly overawed by the evident riches of the city, by the gems and precious metals he saw all around him, and by the fine silks and materials which adorned his lodgings. At the time Commynes was writing, annual receipts to the Venetian treasury were running at about a million gold ducats – roughly a half of the King of France's yearly income. Although Commynes is unlikely to have made this calculation for himself, the evidence of spectacular wealth was all too visible.

Florence also boasted ample riches. Its ruler until 1492, Lorenzo de Medici, was not only the head of one of Europe's largest banking organisations, but was also a famous patron of artists and scholars. Even during his own lifetime he was nicknamed 'The Magnificent'. Of Florence's splendour during the years immediately preceding Charles VIII's invasion, Benedetto Dei wrote:

1 We have round about us 30 000 estates, owned by noblemen and merchants, citizens and craftsmen, yielding in yearly bread and meat, wine and oil, vegetables and cheese, hay and wood, to the value of 900 000 ducats in cash . . . Our beautiful Florence
5 contains within the city in this present year [1472] 270 shops belonging to the wool merchants' guild, from whence their wares are sent to Rome and the Marshes, Naples and Sicily, Constantinople and Pera, Adrianople, Broussa and the whole of Turkey. It contains also 83 rich and splendid warehouses of the silk
10 merchants' guild, and furnishes gold and silver stuffs, velvet, brocade, damask, taffeta and satin to Rome, Naples, Catalonia and the whole of Spain . . . The number of banks amounts to 33; the shops of the cabinet makers, whose business is carving and inlaid work, to 84; and the workshops of the stonecutters and
15 marble workers in the city and its immediate neighbourhood to 54. There are 44 goldsmiths' and jewellers' shops, 30 goldbeaters, silver-wire drawers and a wax-figure maker . . .

Rome, Mantua, Ferrara and the other cities of the north were similarly luxurious. Even the feudal and relatively backward kingdom of Naples had a resplendent royal court, and the heavy taxes which burdened the Neapolitans provided their king with the wherewithal to match his fellow-rulers in princely generosity.

Campaigning abroad was a costly business. Mercenary soldiers needed their wages paid; noble supporters required a constant supply of booty to reward their loyalty. With its riches there for the taking, Italy was an obvious target for invasion. In the early years of the seventeenth century, a French theorist remarked that, 'those who are called to be rulers of states should have glory, expansion and enrichment as their principal aims'. As his armies entered Italy in 1494, Charles VIII must have believed himself about to secure all three objectives at a single stroke.

2 Charles VIII's Expedition

Charles VIII's advance through Italy bore many of the characteristics of a chivalric romance. As the military procession made its way southwards, the local rulers all hurried to come to terms with the King and to assure him of their support. Lodovico Sforza of Milan accompanied Charles along part of the route; Pope Alexander VI and Piero de Medici, ruler of Florence, admitted the King into their territories. Naples itself proved an easy prey. King Ferrante had died earlier in the year. On the approach of the French army, Ferrante's successor, Alfonso, abdicated. Alfonso's son, Ferrante II (Ferrantino) took the throne – and promptly fled. Charles occupied the Neapolitan capital in February 1495 and, a few months later, was crowned King of Naples.

Yet as would happen again in the future, the very extent of the French triumph encouraged the other powers in the peninsula to rally together against what they perceived to be a new threat to their independence. As the contemporary Italian historian, Guicciardini, observed:

1 It has been shown that the desire to usurp the duchy of Milan and Lodovico Sforza's fear of the [Neapolitans] and of Piero de Medici had inclined him to summon the French king into Italy . . . But now a second fear, much more potent and justified than 5 the first, began to present itself before Lodovico's eyes – namely, the imminent servitude of himself and all Italians if the kingdom of Naples should be added to the power of the King of France . . . The same fear began to preoccupy the minds of the Venetian Senate . . . After seeing the vehement course of French good 10 fortune, and how the King was passing through Italy like a thunderbolt without any resistance, the Venetians began to consider the misfortunes of others as dangers to themselves, and to fear that the ruin of others would inevitably involve their own.

In April 1495 the League of Venice was formed with the objective of forcing Charles to disgorge Naples. The principal agents in setting up the League were Venice and Milan, and to their number they added the Pope. Aware that his communications with France were gravely threatened, Charles abandoned his newly-acquired kingdom. Leaving only a garrison in Naples, he began the long march northwards, hoping to reach home before his enemies could cut him off. However, he was caught by the army of the League at Fornovo. His forces suffered a severe mauling there before eventually breaking through to continue their march. Meanwhile, the garrison left behind in Naples was overcome by the League and King Ferrante II was restored. Thus ended the first French expedition to Italy, with a gain to the King of France of precisely nothing.

3 Louis XII

Charles VIII died in 1498 and was succeeded by his distant cousin, Duke Louis of Orléans. Together with the crown of France, Louis inherited Charles VIII's claim to Naples. Additionally Louis believed that his own family had an ancient dynastic right to the duchy of Milan. As it was, the possession of Milan was hotly contested between the family of the previous ruler, Gian Galeazzo, the current despot, Lodovico Sforza, and the Emperor Maximilian, who considered the city-state to be a part of the Empire. Thus, although Milan was closer to France and so more easily controlled than Naples, Louis's claims were bound to meet resistance.

Louis XII prepared for the capture of Milan with a flurry of diplomatic activity. Having allied with the Pope, Venice, the rulers of Spain and the Emperor Maximilian, he invaded the duchy in 1499 and ousted Lodovico Sforza. With French rule over Milan seemingly secure, Louis moved on to his second objective, Naples. In November 1500 he made an alliance with the Spanish King of Sicily, Ferdinand of Aragon. In the Treaty of Granada, the two rulers agreed to split the kingdom of Naples between them, with Louis retaining the northern part and the royal title.

In a rapid campaign of conquest, the kingdom of Naples was simultaneously overrun by French and Aragonese forces, and in 1501 Louis took possession of his Neapolitan inheritance. Even at the time, surprise was expressed at the partition of Naples, which was regarded as the seed of future conflict. As Guicciardini reported:

1   Men's fears were transformed into amazement, everyone finding
    the King of France greatly wanting in prudence, in that he
    preferred rather that half of that realm should fall into the hands
    of the King of Spain, bringing into Italy, where before he had
5   been the sole arbiter of things, another king as his rival, to whom
    all his enemies and those discontented with him might have
    recourse, and furthermore, one who was allied with the King of
    the Romans [Maximilian] by very close interests.

Predictably, Louis and Ferdinand fell out, and within a year they were at war. By 1504 Louis had lost all of the Neapolitan kingdom and was compelled to recognise Aragonese mastery in southern Italy. In the north, however, Louis still remained, as one contemporary put it, 'boss of the shop'.

Over the next few years Louis consolidated his hold on the duchy of Milan, but in 1508 Pope Julius II encouraged Louis to make war on the Venetian republic which had recently been involved in a territorial dispute with the Holy See. In return for joining the League of Cambrai in alliance with the Pope, Maximilian (who had a score to settle with the Venetians, as they had recently taken some imperial possessions on the eastern shore of the Adriatic) and Ferdinand of Aragon (who wanted the Venetian-held ports on the Neapolitan coast), Louis was promised the eastern portions of the plain of Lombardy, presently under Venetian sway.

In the battle of Agnadello (May 1509), the Venetians were routed and division of the spoils followed apace. However, the prospect of Louis substantially augmenting his possessions in north Italy resulted in yet another somersault in relations between the powers. Pope Julius II turned against the French and requested help to expel the 'barbarians' from Italy. When in 1511 Louis retaliated by summoning a Council of the Church to meet at Pisa and making this puppet-body threaten to depose the Pope, Julius organised a 'Holy League' against the French King. With the support of the Venetians, the Swiss, Ferdinand of Aragon and Maximilian, the new coalition swept the French forces before them. After a stunning defeat at Novara (1513), Louis was compelled to evacuate all his forces from the peninsula. Milan was lost and, as the fighting spilled outside the peninsula, much of the French satellite kingdom of Navarre was seized by King Ferdinand. By the time of Louis' death in 1515, the vast expenditure of French effort and manpower on the wars in Italy had still not yielded any fruit.

4 Francis I and the Habsburg–Valois Wars

Louis XII was succeeded by his cousin, Francis of Angoulême (Francis I). By now, the pattern of French military involvement in Italy was so established, and the claims of the kings of France to Milan and Naples so vaunted, as to make it impossible for the new ruler to desist from war. Thus less than six months after his accession, Francis led a new army southwards into Italy and advanced on Milan. In the battle of Marignano (September 1515) the King defeated the Swiss army which the Duke of Milan had called to his aid. As a consequence, Milan passed once more into French hands, and the Swiss were compelled to make an alliance with France (the Perpetual Peace of Fribourg). Additionally, in the Concordat of Bologna (1516) Pope Leo X formally recognised all Francis I's territorial claims in north Italy. Within a year of his accession, Francis enjoyed a stronger position in Italy than any of his forebears.

'His appearance is completely regal, so much so, that without ever having seen his face or his portrait, merely seeing him one would say, 'It is the King'. All his movements are so noble and majestic that no other prince can rival him. His nature is robust despite the excessive fatigues he has always had to endure and which he still has to endure in all his progresses and journeys. There are few men who could bear such hardship . . . He eats and drinks heartily, he sleeps even better and, what is more, he likes to spend his days in pastime and pleasure.'
(The Venetian Marino Cavalli in 1546).
Francis was renowned for his personal courage. Of his valour at the battle of Marignano (1515), the French courtier and diarist, Jean Barrillon, wrote: 'The king did his duty well and did not spare himself. He was struck three times by a pike and his life would have been seriously threatened if he had not been well protected by his armour.'

Portrait of Francis I by Jean Clover (c. 1525)

Francis's confidence and ambition were such that in 1519 he put himself forward as the next Holy Roman Emperor, an elective post made recently vacant by the death of Maximilian. Francis was only narrowly defeated in the contest by Maximilian's grandson, Charles of Habsburg, who forthwith became Emperor Charles V. Charles was the hereditary ruler of the Netherlands and, since 1516, King of Castile, Aragon, Naples and Sicily.

The rapid rise of Charles of Habsburg from relative obscurity in the Netherlands to ruler of half of Europe was to have a major effect both on French foreign policy and on Italian politics. As ruler of Spain, the Netherlands and the Empire, Charles's possessions hemmed France in on two sides: along France's eastern frontier and southwards along the Pyrenees. Francis looked to Italy as the way out of the Habsburg ring. By maintaining a presence in north Italy, Francis hoped to break the encirclement of his kingdom and to allow himself room for manoeuvre on the international stage. Thus the Italian Wars acquired an entirely new significance. Previously the fighting in the peninsula had been caused by the French kings' desire for land and booty. After 1519, the Italian Wars became absorbed within the wider international struggle of Valois *versus* Habsburg.

The quarrel between Francis I and Charles V involved more, however, than political geography. Both rulers nursed grievances against each other. Charles resented in particular the French occupation of Burgundy, a part of eastern France which had belonged to his great-grandfather and which had been taken by Louis XI in 1477. Additionally, Charles regarded Milan as an imperial property and therefore believed it rightfully to be his. Francis in turn objected to the Spanish seizure of Navarre in 1512 and to Charles's possession of territories in the Netherlands and Franche-Comté which technically belonged to the French crown. The rivalry between the two rulers was touched by personal bitterness, and on several occasions, Charles suggested a duel as the best way of resolving their animosity. Francis I, however, always backed away from a face-to-face confrontation. He preferred to pursue the contest in Italy: a land with which he was familiar, where wealthy cities were for the taking, and where he had territorial rights to pursue.

* The first years of Habsburg–Valois rivalry were hidden by the mask of friendship as both rulers sought to outmanoeuvre each other diplomatically. Only in 1521 was the war renewed, when Francis invaded Habsburg Luxembourg. As the fighting spread to Italy, Francis's armies were rapidly overcome and the imperial forces took Milan. A relief force sent the next year by Francis to recapture the city was defeated at the battle of La Bicocca (1522).

Over the following years Francis desperately tried to regain a foothold in the peninsula. The defection of Francis's chief commander, the Constable Bourbon, to Charles's side in 1523 and fear of an English attack into northern France, prevented anything more than incon-

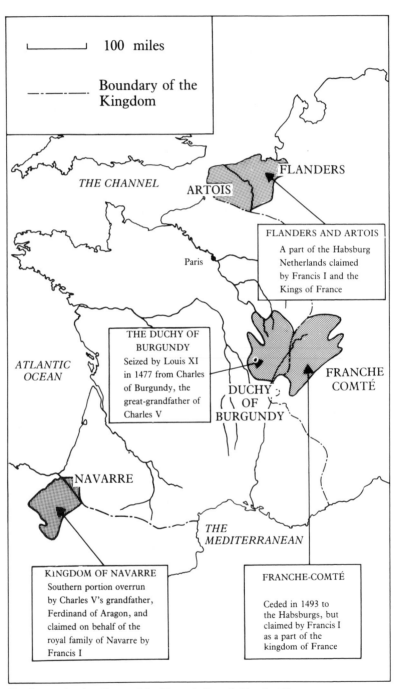

100 miles

Boundary of the Kingdom

THE CHANNEL

FLANDERS

ARTOIS

FLANDERS AND ARTOIS
A part of the Habsburg Netherlands claimed by Francis I and the Kings of France

Paris

THE DUCHY OF BURGUNDY
Seized by Louis XI in 1477 from Charles of Burgundy, the great-grandfather of Charles V

ATLANTIC OCEAN

DUCHY OF BURGUNDY

FRANCHE COMTÉ

NAVARRE

THE MEDITERRANEAN

KINGDOM OF NAVARRE
Southern portion overrun by Charles V's grandfather, Ferdinand of Aragon, and claimed on behalf of the royal family of Navarre by Francis I

FRANCHE-COMTÉ
Ceded in 1493 to the Habsburgs, but claimed by Francis I as a part of the kingdom of France

Border territories disputed by Francis I and Charles V

sequential forays. Only in late 1524 was Francis able to take the field in person. Crossing the Alps in record time, he reoccupied Milan and despatched an army southwards to carry the war into Naples. However, as Francis prepared to besiege the city of Pavia, his forces were caught by Charles's generals. In the battle of Pavia (1525), the French army suffered its greatest defeat for over a century and the King himself was captured.

In the Treaty of Madrid (1526), signed by Francis while a prisoner in the capital of Castile, the King promised to return Burgundy to Charles and to give up all his Italian claims. Once freed, he immediately disavowed these commitments, claiming that they had been extracted from him under duress. The fighting in Italy was thus renewed. In this phase of the conflict, Francis had the support of the rulers of Venice and Florence, the exiled Duke of Milan and the Pope, all of whom were fearful of Charles's great influence in the peninsula. However, the new coalition (joined together in 1526 in the League of Cognac) proved incapable of resisting the awesome might of the Emperor. In 1527 the imperial forces sacked the city of Rome and the coalition broke up in mutual recrimination. An attempt the next year by Francis to capture Naples proved similarly disastrous. His army was cut off, decimated by disease, and forced into a humiliating surrender. In the Peace of Cambrai (1529) Francis was obliged once again formally to renounce all his claims in Italy.

* The Peace of Cambrai marks the end of the Italian Wars. Although Francis managed to conquer the border-duchy of Savoy in 1536, he was never able to regain a foothold in the peninsula. Milan was completely beyond his reach. A Habsburg puppet from the Sforza family was installed in the city. When he died in 1535 Milan was fully absorbed into Charles's personal empire and placed under the command of a lieutenant-general. After the Peace of Cambrai, Venice, Genoa, Florence and the Papacy all sought to come to terms with the Emperor. Habsburg marriage-treaties with their rulers and the imposition of imperial garrisons in their great cities, ensured the continued loyalty of the Italian states. At the same time, new defensive works and ramparts were built around the cities, making them far less vulnerable to assault. Part of the attraction of Italy had always been the speediness with which victories might be won and defiant cities captured. Such new military architecture as Florence's Fortezza da Basso, built in 1534, prevented further campaigns of rapid conquest and ensured that the territorial *status quo* would remain firmly in Charles's favour.

* The end of warfare in Italy did not bring hostilities between Francis I and Charles V to a close. With Italy no longer a theatre of conflict, the Habsburg–Valois wars became 'Europeanised'. Although neither Francis nor his son and successor, Henry II, ever gave up trying to break into Italy, both increasingly sought to harm Charles by stirring up the German princes against him. During the 1530s, therefore,

German engraving of the Battle of Pavia

Francis subsidised the Protestant Schmalkaldic League and funded Charles's enemy, Philip of Hesse. At the same time, Francis allied with Charles's principal foe in the Netherlands, the Protestant duke of Guelders. Later on, in the 1550s, Henry II joined in the Treaty of Chambord (1552) with the rebel Maurice of Saxony, and captured

Metz, Toul and Verdun from the Emperor. Most notoriously, Francis extended the number of his allies to include the Turkish Sultan. In 1536 a formal arrangement was made between Francis and the Ottoman ruler, whereby both agreed to coordinate their campaigns against Charles. Six years later, the alliance was renewed. While Francis fought in the Netherlands, the Ottoman fleet harried the coastline of Italy and Sicily. Subsequently, the Turkish fleet wintered in the French port of Toulon. 30 000 Muslim warriors disembarked on French soil, peaceably establishing their own mosque and slavemarket, to the great shock of Christians everywhere.

The web of alliances spun by Francis advanced his fortunes little. In the continuing conflict between Valois and Habsburg, the King of France was nearly always the loser. Francis did not have sufficient resources to defeat the Emperor and his kingdom might easily be attacked at any of the many places where it adjoined Habsburg territory. In the war of 1536–37, both northern France and Provence were invaded. Between 1542 and 1544, the territories along the border with the Habsburg Netherlands and Luxembourg again proved highly vulnerable. However, the successful capture by Henry II of Metz, Toul and Verdun in 1552 provided some small return for the years of war. But Henry's defeat by Charles's successor, Philip II, at the siege of St Quentin (1557) halted further expansion.

* The Peace of Cateau–Cambrésis (1559), which was negotiated in the aftermath of the defeat at St Quentin, marks the end of the Habsburg–Valois wars. According to the terms of this treaty, Henry II resigned all his claims to Habsburg territories and recognised Philip II's superior rights in Italy and the Netherlands. Additionally, the duchy of Savoy, occupied by Francis I in 1536, was returned to its legitimate ruler. Calais, however, seized from Philip II's English ally in 1558, remained French, along with Metz, Toul and Verdun.

As the terms of the Peace of Cateau–Cambrésis suggest, the Italian and Habsburg wars produced little tangible benefit for the Kings of France. By 1559, the boundary of the kingdom was virtually the same as it had been in 1494. True, Metz, Toul, Verdun and Calais had been won; but against these gains must be set the loss of Navarre in 1512. Seen in this light, the protracted struggle must appear one of the most fruitless episodes in the whole of French history. Furthermore, and as we will see in Chapter 4, the vast expenditure of French resources and manpower in these foreign wars exhausted the kingdom and was partly responsible for the outbreak of civil war in 1562. Thus the wars of 1494–1559 not only failed to bring any significant gain, but also proved harmful to France's internal stability.

In many respects, however, a balance-sheet of territorial gains and losses is a poor way to judge the military deeds of Charles VIII, Louis XII, Francis I and Henry II. During the medieval and early modern periods, warfare was regarded as an inescapable feature of international

Marino Cavalli described Henry II in 1546 as, 'of very robust constitution, but somewhat melancholy in humour. He is very skilled in the use of arms. He is not a good conversationalist, but very clear and firm in his opinions – what he has once said, he holds to stubbornly. He is of mediocre intelligence, slow to react.'

The eighteenth-century French historian, J-A De Thou, wrote of Henry II, 'He loved war and seized with joy every opportunity of taking up arms. Otherwise, he was kind and easy-going and tended to follow the ideas of others rather than his own sentiments'.

Portrait of Henry II by Primaticcio

politics and was considered a praiseworthy objective in its own right. As a Venetian commentator was later to write, 'War is the real calling of a Great Captain and King'. Simply by fighting abroad, regardless of defeat or cost, the kings of France were fulfilling one of their principal obligations. Thus, if we condemn them for their folly, we must condemn also the whole age and ethos in which they lived and in which they practised this 'sport of kings'.

5 Warfare

In reviewing military developments during his own lifetime, Francesco Guicciardini wrote:

1 In our own age methods of warfare have undergone the greatest change: in that before King Charles of France marched into Italy the brunt of battle was borne much more by horsemen heavily armoured at all points, than by footsoldiers; and since the
5 weapons that were used against the towns were very difficult to move and manage, therefore, although armies frequently engaged in battles, there was very little killing, and most rare was the blood that was shed, and the cities under attack defended themselves so easily (not because of skilful defence but because of
10 the lack of skill of the attack) that there was no town so small or so weak that it could not hold out for many days against the greatest armies of their enemies; with the result that only with the greatest difficulties could one make armed seizure of states belonging to others.
15 But after King Charles had come to Italy, the terror of unknown nations, the ferocity of infantry organised in waging war in another way, but above all, the fury of the artillery, filled all of Italy with so much dread that no hope of defending oneself remained for those not powerful enough to resist in the
20 countryside; for men who were unskilled in defending their towns surrendered as soon as the enemy approached, and even if some put up resistance, they were taken within a very few days. Thus the kingdom of Naples and the duchy of Milan were attacked and conquered almost in a single day; thus the
25 Venetians, beaten in one battle only, abandoned the entire empire they had on the mainland; thus the French, having scarcely seen their enemies left the duchy of Milan. Thus terrified by the ferocity of the attacks, men began to whet their wits and contrive more subtle means of defence, fortifying
30 their towns with banks, ditches, moats, flanks, ramparts and bastions: whence the towns now being defended have been made safe and cannot be taken by storm.

Although Guicciardini doubtless exaggerates the bloodlessness of the fighting in Italy before Charles VIII's invasion, his account accurately summarises the principal changes in warfare over the period which followed.

The rapidity of Charles VIII's and Louis XII's conquests of Milan and Naples owed much to their use of artillery: huge bronze cannons and siege-guns capable of firing iron balls (not given like stone balls to shattering on impact) and dragged into place by teams of horses. The French artillery rapidly reduced the thin shell walls which protected the cities of Italy. As Charles VIII recorded in a dispatch while *en route* to Naples:

1   Today [4 February 1495] I besieged one of the strongest places in
    this whole region, both for its defences and its situation. It is
    called Monte San Giovanni . . . My cousin Montpensier had
    arrived before me with my artillery . . . and after firing for four
5   hours my said artillery had made a breach wide enough for an
    assault. I ordered it to be made by men-at-arms and others, and
    though the place was held by 5–600 good fighting men as well as
    its inhabitants, they went in in such a manner that, thanks to
    God, [the town] has been taken with little loss to me, and to the
10 inhabitants great loss, punishment and great example to those
    others who might think of obstructing me.

The revolutionary effect of artillery on methods of fighting cannot be overstated. As the account given above suggests, heavy siege-guns speeded up the process of conquest. In the context of the Italian Wars, this only made campaigning more attractive by extending the prospect of speedy victories. However, as Guicciardini makes clear, military architecture soon evolved to meet the artillery's challenge. During the early years of the sixteenth century, and more particularly during the 1530s, fortifications were built specifically to resist the impact of the cannon. In the main, the new fortifications assumed the form of ramparts and bastions: very thick, brick walls from which projected angular platforms. In front of the bastions stretched ditches and elevations designed to impede frontal assaults.

The development of defensive works robbed the cannon of its military ascendancy. Sieges became, therefore, long, drawn-out affairs spread over many months. As more and more cities both in Italy and elsewhere in Europe acquired new ramparts, campaigning was reduced to a seemingly endless round of blockades. More than any other, it is this feature of sixteenth-century warfare which explains the indecisive nature of the Habsburg–Valois wars in the period after 1529. Neither side had the time nor the manpower to overrun the obstacles put in its way and to wage a campaign deep in enemy territory. The borders of both France and the Netherlands were guarded by chains of strongly-fortified towns: Doullens, La Capelle, Thérouanne, Charlemont, Philippeville and Mariembourg. The Italian cities were similarly well defended, with Florence, Rome and Milan all acquiring new walls. As siegework became the norm, the set-piece battle became the exception. Whereas in the early years of the Italian and Habsburg wars, decisive engagements on open ground had been commonplace – Fornovo, Agnadello, Marignano, La Bicocca, Pavia – field-battles were seldom fought after the 1520s. The charge thus gave way to the salvo, the lance to the spade.

   * The time required to capture one of the newly-fortified towns encourged the numerical growth of the infantry and put a premium on ever-larger armies. This tendency was hastened by the development of the arcquebus (a primitive musket) and by the use of the pike, both of which were infantry weapons. Battlefield strategy became largely a matter of blocks of infantry firing at each other and giving cover to the pikemen as they advanced to skewer and drive away their opponents. In such circumstances, gallant charges and cunning manoeuvres were increasingly irrelevant. Victory went instead to him who had the most arcquebusiers and pikemen. Whereas Charles VIII had invaded Italy in 1494 with 28 000 men, for the assault on Metz in 1552 Henry II employed about 40 000 troops, in the main pike- and gun-men.

   The growth of infantry armies saw a corresponding decline in the number of the cavalry. Against pikes in particular, horsemen were quite useless, seldom being able to close with the enemy. Accordingly, the cavalry were reduced in number and used only as skirmishers or as a reserve. In 1494 cavalry had made up almost a half of Charles VIII's army. By the time of the battle of Pavia (1525) they comprised only a fifth of the royal forces.

   Traditionally, the core of the French army comprised of noblemen. The nobles fought on horseback, and they provided their own chargers, armour and retainers. In the main the nobles volunteered for service, but in time of war they could be compelled to honour their military obligations to the King and to provide assistance virtually free of charge. Trained in the jousting-pens and accustomed by hunting to long hours in the saddle, the nobility provided an experienced and relatively cheap source of warriors.

   The kingdom of France, however, was not so well equipped with reliable infantrymen. Although native volunteers might be found, these were in the main ill-disciplined. Most lacked the training to hold a pike in the heat of battle or to discharge an arcquebus with accuracy. Consequently, the kings of France had to rely upon the services of professional footsoldiers, especially Swiss and German mercenaries.

   Mercenaries required payment and owed their loyalty to the highest bidder. As one of Francis's commanders reported, while negotiating with the Swiss captains, 'These people ask for so much money and are so unreasonable that it is almost impossible to satisfy them'. Yet if he wanted to continue fighting abroad, Francis had to satisfy the mercenaries' 'unreasonableness'. As Francis's need for infantrymen grew, the cost of mercenary-recruitment escalated. Thus whereas in the first years of his reign, Francis's annual expenditure on troops was less than two million *livres*, by 1544 he was spending six million *livres*. Under his successor, the figure doubled again. As we will see in the next chapter, the cost of war was to have important consequences for French domestic history.

Making Notes on 'The Italian and Habsburg–Valois Wars'

In noting this chapter, be careful not to allow what you write to become so cluttered with detail as to make it incomprehensible. As you read, jot down a brief date-chart so as to help you remember the basic chronology of events. In your notes you should give special consideration to the motives of the French kings, and to the reasons why they were unable to fulfil their ambitions abroad. Try and avoid making a condensed narrative survey – leave this to your date-chart. The following headings and questions should help you make notes:

1.   Origins
1.1. Charles VIII's claims in Italy
1.2. Political fragmentation
1.3. Wealth
2.   Charles VIII's expedition.
       In this section you have read about how a primitive 'balance of power' operated in Italian politics. As you continue the chapter, note carefully additional instances when alliances were formed in order to stop any one power in the peninsula enjoying a monopoly of influence.
3.   Louis XII
4.   Francis I and the Habsburg–Valois wars
4.1. Habsburg–Valois rivalry
4.2. Defeat in Italy
4.3. Italy after the Peace of Cambrai
4.4. The European conflict
4.5. The Peace of Cateau–Cambrésis
5.   Warfare
5.1. The importance of artillery
5.2. The growth of the infantry
       To what extent did military development during this period contribute to France's failure abroad?

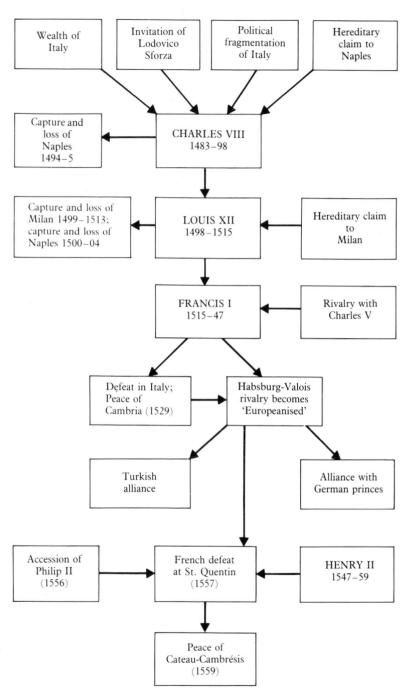

Summary of The Italian and Habsburg – Valois wars 1494–1559

Answering essay-questions on _'The Italian and Habsburg–Valois Wars'_

Questions on the Italian and Habsburg–Valois wars will usually ask you to explain why they were fought and why they lasted so long. You will never be asked to give a simple account of the wars, so there is no need to learn every detail of the fighting. Occasionally, the questions will be quite straightforward, for example:

> 'Why was Italy the theatre of so much conflict in the period after 1494?'

> 'Why was the fighting between the Habsburg and Valois rulers of Europe so prolonged?'

When meeting questions beginning with a 'Why?', construct a plan consisting of clauses beginning with 'Because'. A plan for the first question might read:

> – Because of the claims of the French kings to parts of Italy.
> – Because other European rulers were also interested in extending their influence in Italy.
> – Because of the wealth of the Italian cities.
> – Because after 1519 France was surrounded by Habsburg possessions, and Italy was the way out of her encirclement.

In writing your essay, expand each of these clauses into full paragraphs, including plenty of detail to reinforce your point-of-view. In developing the first clause, for instance, you could refer to the claims of Charles VIII to Naples and of Louis XII to Milan. In your conclusion, summarise what you have written in a series of short sentences.

Often, though, the question will be put in such a way as to rule out such a simple solution:

> '"The involvement of the kings of France in Italy after 1494 was occasioned less by dynastic rights than by a lust for booty and adventure". Discuss.'

The quotation given here needs to be broken down into its component parts and rephrased before you can even think what to write.

If you look at it closely, the question really consists of a series of separate statements:

> – The French kings did not become involved in Italy because they had dynastic rights there.

- They became involved because of their lust for booty and adventure.

and, by implication,

- No other factors were of much significance.

By breaking the question down into its parts, a method for tackling it emerges. Your essay can now be divided into three sections, each of which considers the arguments for and against the three statements given above. Thus, your first paragraph could outline the dynastic rights which the French kings had in Italy and explain the importance attached to these. The second could discuss the opportunities for a glorious and profitable war, and the third could explain what other reasons the kings of France might have had for fighting in the peninsula.

Questions with a quotation in them will nearly always need to be 'unpacked' in this manner. Once you have broken them down their meaning will become apparent and a way of answering the question will usually emerge. In exams, such careful consideration of the essay title will require a steely nerve. However, the five minutes or so spent in preparation and planning will improve the structure and flow of your essay quite considerably. By cutting out the possibility of irrelevant and rambling paragraphs, such forethought may actually save you time in the long-run.

Please note that in exam questions 'Italian Wars' is sometimes (and quite misleadingly) used as a catch-all term for the entire conflict of 1494–1559. Watch, therefore, the dates given in the essay title very carefully. If 'Italian Wars' is used without any date being given at all, you may either stop at 1529, explaining why you have done so, or go on *briefly* to 1559. The term 'Habsburg–Valois Wars' can refer only, of course, to the conflict fought between 1519 and 1559.

Source-based questions on the *'Italian and Habsburg–Valois Wars'*

1 Charles VIII and the French intervention in Italy
Read the extract from the memoirs of Commynes on page 11, the Florentine ambassador's statement on page 13, and the description of Florence given by Benedetto Dei on page 14. Answer the following questions:
a) According to Commynes, what prompted Charles VIII to turn his attention to Italian affairs?
b) Whom does the Florentine ambassador hold responsible for the

wars in Italy? What historical evidence might be put forward to support the ambassador's point-of-view?

c) What, on the basis of Benedetto Dei's account, may be presumed to be the principal sources of Florence's wealth in the period preceding Charles VIII's invasion?

2 Charles VIII and Louis XII

Read the accounts written by Guicciardini on pages 15 and 16. Answer the following questions:

a) Explain the circumstances of Lodovico Sforza's decision to invite Charles VIII into Italy.

b) To what extent is Guicciardini correct in suggesting that Louis XII undermined his position in Italy by inviting Ferdinand of Aragon to participate in the partition of Naples?

c) Using these sources and any other evidence known to you, examine the extent to which the kings of France may be said to have failed in Italy as a consequence of their own reckless ambition.

3 Warfare

Read the account given by Guicciardini on page 25, and the text of Charles VIII's despatch on page 26. Look at the picture of the battle of Pavia on page 22. Answer the following:

a) In what ways does Charles VIII's despatch confirm Guicciardini's account of military developments in this period?

b) How according to Guicciardini did military architecture evolve to meet the new defensive requirements imposed by the use of artillery? To what extent does your own knowledge of changes in military fortification during this period support Guicciardini's assessment?

c) How might the military changes mentioned by Guicciardini have led to the growth in size of infantry armies? What other developments, as depicted in the illustration of the battle of Pavia, may have hastened this process?

4 The Personalities of Francis I and Henry II

Read the accounts of Francis I given by Marino Cavalli and Jean Barrillon, and look at the portrait of Francis I on page 18. Read the accounts of Henry II given by Cavalli and De Thou, and look at the portrait of Henry II on page 24. Answer the following questions:

a) To what extent does Barrillon's short account confirm the opinion of Marino Cavalli concerning Francis I? Which of these two sources is likely to contain the more accurate assessment of the king? Explain your choice.

b) In what ways does De Thou's opinion of Henry II coincide with the earlier assessment provided by Marino Cavalli? Under what circumstances should we believe the verdict of a historian to be more accurate than the opinion of a contemporary writer?

c) Sixteenth-century painters of royal portraits deliberately emphasised the magnificence and bearing of their subjects. In what ways might these two portraits be considered typical?

CHAPTER 3

French Renaissance Monarchy

1 The Growth of Royal Government

Some years ago historians of early modern Europe wrote much about 'New' or 'Renaissance Monarchy'. 'New Monarchy' was the term used to describe the type of government which emerged in the sixteenth century and which was believed to lie halfway between the feudal monarchy of the middle ages and the absolute monarchy of the seventeenth century. During the period of New Monarchy, so it was argued, the power of the monarch steadily grew as he extended his sway over those local organisations of law and justice which had developed during the middle ages. As a consequence of this development, the almost independent rights belonging to towns, feudal landowners and regional assemblies were drastically curtailed. Ferdinand and Isabella of Spain, Henry VII of England and Gustavus Vasa of Sweden were all considered to be typical New Monarchs.

Although as a historical concept, New Monarchy survived rather longer than most, it has few supporters nowadays. After all, the steady accumulation of power by the ruler is as much a feature of the middle ages as of the sixteenth century. Additionally, 'medieval' institutions may be shown to have had a remarkable capacity for endurance, with many surviving until well into the modern period. Nevertheless, despite its unfashionability, New Monarchy lingers on in historical writing, although usually under the alternative name of 'Renaissance Monarchy'.

For all their faults, New Monarchy or Renaissance Monarchy are still useful expressions, providing they are not applied too dogmatically. During the sixteenth century there was an undoubted shift towards the 'stronger state'. Throughout western Europe, royal government expanded well beyond the limits set in the middle ages. Overmighty subjects were brought to heel, and the King's officials enforced his commands with new vigour and success. In most states, however, this development encountered obstacles, put up in the main by those privileged groups which felt the most threatened by an expansion of royal authority. Invariably, the crown compromised with the forces of obstruction. The resulting accommodation left the administrative chaos of competing institutions which characterises the eighteenth-century *Ancien Régime*.

The spur towards the 'stronger state' was the King's need for ever larger sums of cash, in the main to pay for mercenary armies. In the period of French Renaissance Monarchy, we may note a direct link between financial necessity and the growth of a more powerful and centralised government. This is not to say that the drive towards greater royal control was lacking in the fifteenth century. The cost of war simply hastened a trend which was already developing.

* By the last years of the fifteenth century, annual royal income and expenditure were roughly balanced in France at between two and three million *livres*. French involvement in the Italian Wars rapidly upset the financial equation. Shortly after Francis I's accession, the crown was in debt to the tune of four million *livres*. In order to ease the treasury of this burden, new sources of income had to be found. These, however, provided only temporary relief, for costs continued to rise. By the time of Francis's death in 1547 the amount needed to field an army abroad far exceeded the crown's resources. Thus additional ways of raising money had to be found, and when these proved insufficient, debts had to be taken on. By 1559 the crown owed 12 million *livres* on which it was unable to pay even the interest charges.

Imposing heavier taxes was one obvious way for the King to increase his income. During the first half of the century, the *taille* doubled in value and the *gabelle* may even have tripled. However, the overall increase in taxation barely kept pace with inflation. In order to make up for the shortfall, the kings of France began to sell offices of the crown. Purchasers of crown offices had the right to administer parts of the royal judicial and financial apparatus, and to take what profit they could from their activities. Crown offices also gave their owner noble rank and provided exemption from certain taxes. Thus they were eagerly purchased by 'upwardly-mobile' members of the *bourgeoisie*.

The spread of venality, as the sale of offices is known, gathered pace as the King's need for money grew. Louis XI and Charles VIII first sold offices in the financial administration; Louis XII extended the practice to posts in the judicial service. In 1524 a special department was set up to administer the income from the sale of offices and Francis I began to create unnecessary posts with the sole intention of putting them up for auction. During the reign of Francis's successor, the spread of useless offices became rampant. Henry II appointed, for instance, forestry officials to administer areas where there were no forests at all, and he set up an entirely new layer of superfluous judicial posts. Between 1515 and 1559 the number of royal office-holders doubled. Income from the sale of posts reached about 1.5 million *livres* by the middle of the century.

At the same time as they were creating and selling offices, the kings of France refined their methods of borrowing money. Francis I was the first to raise cash through *rentes sur l'hôtel de ville de Paris*; interest-bearing bonds which were guaranteed by the Paris city-council. The backing of the municipality of Paris made these bonds attractive to private investors and allowed the King to tap new sources of wealth. Banking syndicates were additionally involved in funding the royal debt and in providing new sources of credit. A number of bankers and financiers also bought the right to collect taxes in certain parts of the kingdom. The sale of the right to collect taxes, known as tax-farming, had some advantages for the King. It provided him with an immediate cash-sum and meant that he did not burden his officials with the business of collecting taxpayers' money.

* Although venality and tax-farming put large parts of the royal financial and judicial administration in the hands of private individuals, vigorous rulers like Francis I and Henry II still managed to keep a firm grip on the government of the realm. Royally-appointed officials (led by the *maîtres des requêtes*) supervised the 'privatised' parts of the administration and a hierarchy of courts investigated abuses. In 1523 Francis set up the famous *Commission de la Tour Carrée* to examine the accounts of the realm. The commission's findings resulted in the dismissal of a number of notables who over the preceding years had built up their own private financial empires. At the same time, Francis reorganised the kingdom's chaotic apparatus for raising money, and established a central treasury, the *Épargne*, which was given authority over the entire system of revenue-collection. In the 1560s, the authority of the *Épargne* was superseded by a new officer, 'Superintendent of Finances', who controlled the whole of the realm's financial organisation.

Closely associated with the development of a more centralised financial administration was the emergence of a professional bureaucracy. During the reigns of Francis I and Henry II more and more government business was dealt with by the royal secretaries and notaries, a corps of about 120 officials trained in the law and attached to the royal council. In 1547 Henry II appointed four secretaries to the new office of 'secretary of state' and allowed them to attend meetings of the council. The secretaries of state added their own specialised knowledge and a new measure of administrative coordination to the informal methods of government which had developed in the middle ages. Additionally, as one historian (N.M. Sutherland) has argued, the secretaries of state provided a vital element of continuity in the business of royal government and, at times of great political upheaval, they helped preserve administrative stability.

* The trend towards administrative centralisation rapidly came into conflict with the agencies of local government which had developed during the middle ages. To the great irritation of the kings of France, the many towns and provincial estates of the realm not only obstructed royal officials in the collection of revenues, but also claimed the right to negotiate how much tax they should pay to the crown. From the late fifteenth century onwards, and particularly during Francis I's reign, the independent rights claimed by the towns and provincial assemblies were gradually whittled away. In 1515 Francis set up a body of commissioners to investigate urban finances and to assess what level of taxes the citizens could bear. Shortly afterwards, royal officials (*élus*) were instructed to inquire into the credentials of all organisations and

individuals claiming exemption from taxation. As a royal order of 1517 laid down:

1 In so far as certain towns in our kingdom, certain places, colleges and communities and also certain individuals, including our officers as well as others, claim to be free and exempt from the payment of *tailles* and *gabelles*, we ordain that in all towns, places,
5 colleges, our officers and other individuals shall be subject to the payment of the *tailles*, the strong supporting the weak, with the exception of those who by royal ordinance or by special immunity
. . . are exempt; and we direct our *élus* to compel those who claim privilege to show and demonstrate their immunity and in the case
10 of those whose claims have not been duly and adequately verified and registered in the courts, to subject them to payment of the *tailles*, just like other non-privileged individuals . . .

The provincial estates, the financial jurisdiction of which covered almost half the kingdom, had traditionally bargained with the King over how much tax their regions ought to bear. As the King's financial needs grew, the provincial estates were summoned more often to discuss matters of taxation. In some regions the estates met annually. Despite the frequency of their assemblies, the estates were unable to extract any concessions from the King in return for voting him money. In the majority of cases the estates were notified in advance of the sum which the King required, as this extract from an instruction given in 1515 makes clear:

1 Francis by the Grace of God King of France, to our trusting and well-beloved . . . subjects in the three estates of our land and duchy of Burgundy . . . Having considered the advice of the princes of the blood and of members of our royal council, we have
5 written to instruct you to assemble in our town of Dijon on the twentieth of March next, in order that the state of affairs may be explained to you and a request made to you on our behalf generously to grant and bestow on this occasion the sum of 60 000 *livres* . . .

When a few provincial estates objected to the heavy demands laid upon them, they were browbeaten into submission. In 1517, for instance, the spokesman of the Normandy estates was prosecuted on account of his opposition to an increase in taxes. Elsewhere, royal commissioners were sent in to collect revenues which the estates had either refused to sanction or of which they had not even been notified. By the end of Francis's reign, only three of the provincial estates still had any control of their region's budget. Everywhere else, royal officials were allocating and collecting taxes, in defiance of the estates' traditional authority.

* A similar disregard for local rights and privileges characterised the crown's dealings with the *parlements*. The *parlements*' complaints about financial abuses were repeatedly ignored by the King and administrative reforms were undertaken despite the *parlements*' objections. In 1518 Francis threatened the Paris *parlement* that unless it gave way to him, he would evict it from its premises in the capital and attach it permanently to the royal court: a device which would have left the *parlement* 'trotting after the king', as Francis put it. In 1540 Francis closed down the *parlement* of Rouen altogether when it failed to register a royal edict. For refusing a forced loan, the magistrates of the Bordeaux *parlement* were imprisoned.

By the middle years of the sixteenth century, the authority and power of the French crown stood at an unprecedented height. The towns, provincial estates and *parlements* had been largely forced to give way to the king's constant demand for more money. The administrative system had been reformed, and a greater degree of centralisation obtained. A professional bureaucracy was beginning to appear which was committed to the proper management of the King's resources. Even such potentially damaging devices as the sale of offices and tax-farming were regulated so as to prevent too great a diminution of royal authority. In many respects, therefore, developments in sixteenth-century France would appear to lend support to the New Monarchy thesis. Nevertheless, forces were still present within the kingdom which threatened, if unchecked, to convey the realm back into a condition of administrative disunity and of internal conflict. The two most important of these forces were the tradition of royal consultation and the institution of the governors.

2 Limitations on Royal Authority

Throughout the sixteenth century, the Kings of France maintained the idea that the monarchy was fundamentally consultative in nature. All royal laws and decrees were therefore prefaced with a statement to the effect that the King had taken the opinion of the realm's most important men in devising his latest measures. In nearly all cases, the King had actually done so and his words were not empty rhetoric. The extent to which the King heeded the advice given to him naturally varied.

The most frequently used instrument for taking advice was the royal council. But because the council consisted of only a few persons, usually great lords selected at will, it was customary for the King to consult other bodies when important decisions had to be made. During the middle ages, the Estates-General, the French parliament, had often been summoned to give its opinion in weighty matters. The inability of this body to do much else than complain, eventually obliged the kings of France to turn elsewhere for advice. During the sixteenth century, therefore, assemblies of 'notables' became a more common event. These were meetings of leading noblemen, clergy and officers of the realm at which the King tried to discover the prevailing opinion regarding the course of royal policy.

In order to take account of opinion in the provinces, the kings of France relied on the *parlements*, estates and, to a lesser extent, municipal councils. These were, of course, the same bodies as were proving the greatest obstacle to financial and administrative centralisation. Nevertheless, in their 'remonstrances' (recommendations, usually critical of royal policy) and in their *cahiers* (books of grievances), these local organisations provided the monarch with advice which he was bound to take into account. Indeed, it was still widely felt in the sixteenth century that a royal decree which had been issued without such advice having been sought was of doubtful legal validity.

The requirement of consultation obliged the kings of France to preserve institutions which had no place in a uniform system of royal administration. The *parlements* and the provincial estates jealously guarded their powers and they resented the increased authority of the crown. The logical step for the kings of France would have been to abolish these institutions outright and to fill any resulting administrative gaps with royally-appointed officials. However, the consultative tradition ruled out such far-reaching reform. Thus, the proud institutions of French local government remained in existence, ever ready to reclaim their lost powers should royal authority show signs of faltering.

* The aristocracy might no longer be the King's chief warriors and the main providers of armies. Nevertheless, they continued to be the principal 'recruiting managers' and commanders in the field. In recognition of their important military role, during the late fifteenth and early sixteenth centuries the leading noblemen of the kingdom were given 'governorships' in the frontier provinces. The task of the governors was to provide a coordinated response in the event of invasion.

Under Francis I the number of governors was increased from eleven to sixteen and their powers were extended. Many governors received permission on appointment to set themselves up as virtually independent rulers. Such blanket clauses as allowed individual governors 'generally to do all that we [the King] would see and recognise as necessary for the good of ourself and of our affairs' gave them almost dictatorial powers. During Francis's reign, governorships also became hereditary, thus allowing individual aristocratic families to consolidate their influence over several generations.

Once established as governors, the aristocratic leaders swiftly built up a personal following in the regions under their control. Many nobles voluntarily submitted to the governors, offering them their allegiance in return for favours. Across France, associations of noblemen gathered together, bound in the service of an aristocratic patron. This development was recognised as potentially dangerous by the kings of France, but few determined attempts were made to limit the growing powers of the royal governors. The kings of France believed that the personal loyalty owed to them by the great nobles of France was sufficient to ensure their continued cooperation. Furthermore, neither Francis I nor Henry II had any wish to compromise their good relations with the aristocracy by confiscating powers to which they had become accustomed.

The institution of the governorship confirms the contradictory nature of developments in French government during this period. On the one hand, as royal expenditure exploded to meet the cost of mercenary armies, new administrative methods had to be found. These invariably prompted a greater degree of centralisation and the extension of royal authority over local organisations. However, this tendency was constrained first by the consultative tradition of French monarchy and, secondly, by the crown's continued reliance on the great nobility. As the aristocratic leaders gained new power and prestige through governorships, the possibility of them challenging the revived authority of the crown increased. And when this eventually happened, following the death of Henry II, waiting in the wings were the provincial estates, *parlements* and municipal councils, all anxious to recover what they had lost to the crown during the preceding half-century.

3 Religion and Heresy

The coronation ceremony of the kings of France symbolised the intimate relationship between religion and monarchy. At his coronation the new King was anointed with a 'celestial balm' in a ceremony which deliberately imitated the consecration of a bishop. On the King's head was set the crown of the realm which contained within it a relic of Christ's own Crown of Thorns. By virtue of his anointment and coronation, the King acquired, in the words of one medieval theorist, 'purity and sanctity'. He became a 'holy man', 'a saint', and 'the Most Christian King'. As a mark of his unique status, the King was allegedly able to heal certain diseases with the touch of his hand; and unlike any other layman he could partake of both the bread and the wine during the celebration of Holy Mass. Although he lacked the power to transform the sacraments into the actual body and blood of Christ, the King of France was regarded as being in all other respects the incarnation of the Biblical Melchizedech – he who was 'both priest and King'.

At his coronation, the King solemnly swore to the assembled prelates that he would maintain the Catholic Church:

1 I promise and give you my word that I will scrupulously uphold

the canonical privileges, due authority and jurisdiction belonging
to each of you and to the churches in your keeping, that I will
defend and protect you, with God's help, to the best of my ability,
5 according to the obligation which the King owes every bishop and
church in his kingdom.

* Throughout the middle ages the kings of France acted as if their
solemn obligation to defend the church gave them the right to act as
they wished in the ecclesiastical affairs of the realm. When in 1302 Pope
Boniface VIII reminded Philip IV of France that the Pope in fact
possessed a superior authority over the church, the King had Boniface
violently seized and taken prisoner. Over the following century and a
half, Philip IV's successors took advantage of a long period of papal
weakness to extract recognition from Rome of their extensive powers in
church affairs. The most famous concession wrung out of the Curia was
the Pragmatic Sanction of Bourges (1438) by which all appointments of
bishops and abbots in France were made subject to election, with local
cathedral and monastic chapters choosing whom they wanted at their
head. Since the kings of France could rig elections with little difficulty,
the Pragmatic Sanction left the monarch effective master of the French
church.

Francis I's military involvement in Italy and his need to win an
alliance with the Pope, caused the Pragmatic Sanction to be revised in
1516. The resulting Concordat of Bologna scrapped the practice of
election altogether, substituting for it royal nomination and papal
investiture. This ingenious compromise allowed Francis to control
appointments as before, while granting the Pope a symbolic authority
over the French church. According to the terms of the Concordat, the
Pope agreed that:

1 Henceforward in the case of vacancies now and in the future, in
cathedral and metropolitan churches of the said kingdom . . . the
chapters and monks of these churches may not proceed to the
election or postulation of the future prelate. In the event of such a
5 vacancy whoever is King of France shall within six months
counting from the day on which the vacancy occurred present and
nominate to us and to our successive bishops of Rome a sober or
knowledgeable master or graduate in theology, or a doctor or
graduate in all or in one of the laws taught and rigorously
10 examined at a famous university, who must be at least twenty-
seven years old and otherwise suitable . . . And should the King
not nominate a person with such qualifications, neither we nor
our successors nor the Holy See shall have to invest such a person.
And as regards monasteries and conventual priories . . . in the
15 case of present and future vacancies . . . the monasteries may not
henceforth proceed to the election or postulation of abbots or

priors; when a vacancy occurs the King must make the nomination and the person thus nominated to the vacant monastery will be invested by us and our successors. And the
20 priories will be similarly conferred upon persons nominated by the King . . .

The Concordat of Bologna gave the King control over the appointment of about a hundred bishops and archbishops and of about five hundred abbots and priors. This enormous power of preferment ensured that the French church hierarchy would be a pliant instrument in the King's hands. Few objections were thus raised when Francis I began selling off church property, and when he demanded 'free gifts' of money from the clergy. Within only a short time, even the detailed provisions of the Concordat were overlooked as Francis used church offices to reward his supporters. The ecclesiastical hierarchy was thus absorbed within the structure of royal patronage, and it became exceptional for any bishop or abbot to have the qualifications required by the Concordat.

The extensive powers which the kings of France had over the French church explain their steadfast refusal to break with Rome and to support the Protestant Reformation. The vast majority of European rulers who became Protestant did so primarily in order to justify their confiscation of ecclesiastical property and to set themselves up at the head of a state-church. The Pragmatic Sanction and the 1516 Concordat allowed the French King sufficient control of the church to make the Reformation politically unnecessary. Additionally, by virtue of their coronation oath and of the religious mystique of royalty, the French kings believed they had a moral obligation to resist the spread of heretical ideas.

* Francis I's reign coincided with the opening stages of the Protestant Reformation. Throughout his lifetime, Francis firmly opposed heresy. The main difficulty which he experienced, however, was to discover what actually constituted heresy. Until the middle years of the sixteenth century, the Catholic Church was quite unable to give a precise definition of orthodox belief. Catholic doctrines were unclear. Many leading churchmen had questioned such apparently fundamental ideas as papal supremacy and justification by works – and they were able to find plenty of support for their views in the writings of the Church Fathers, in the records of Church Councils and in the pronouncements of previous popes. In France, in particular, there were many humanists and scholars who, even before the Reformation, had developed theological ideas similar to those later taken up by Protestant thinkers. On the whole, Francis was sympathetic to their ideas and he encouraged them in their work.

The condemnation of Lutheran theology by Pope Leo X in 1521 put Francis in a quandary. Luther was a declared heretic and Francis felt obliged to prevent his ideas from contaminating France. However, because heresy was so ill-defined, humanist critics of the Church might be caught up in a general wave of persecution and unjustly punished. Throughout the 1520s, therefore, Francis adopted a tolerant attitude towards religious dissent, and he regularly intervened to protect critics of the Church from persecution by the Paris *parlement* and the Sorbonne (the influential theological faculty of Paris university). Only in extreme cases, usually involving iconoclasm (the destruction of ceremonial items), did Francis urge the persecution of religious offenders.

Partly as a consequence of royal laxity, Reformation ideas spread in France with little impediment. 'In a certain part of Normandy', wrote the Protestant Martin Bucer, 'the number of those professing the Gospel is so great that their enemies begin to call it a little Germany.' Huge quantities of Lutheran publications were imported from Germany. A bookseller responsible for one shipment was delighted at their reception: 'They are sold in Paris and are read even at the Sorbonne; they meet with everyone's approval'. Many of the printing-presses operating in France also churned out Protestant books, largely untroubled by the authorities. Although we have no way of establishing the number of Protestant converts in the 1520s, the ready market for Lutheran texts suggests a widespread sympathy and interest in Reformation ideas.

* The king's attitude towards religious dissent changed rapidly in the autumn of 1534. On 18 October of that year, in the so-called 'Day of the Placards', posters were stuck up on walls in Paris, in five provincial towns, and even within the precincts of the royal palace. The posters contained an unambiguously heretical message and they poured scorn on the celebration of the Mass. The anonymous author of the posters wrote:

1 I call on Heaven and Earth to bear witness to the truth against this pompous and proud papal Mass by which the world (unless God soon provides a remedy) is being and will be completely destroyed, and in which Our Lord is so outrageously blasphemed
5 and the people seduced and blinded. This can no longer be tolerated . . . Through this wretched Mass almost everyone is being led into public idolatry, for it is falsely claimed that Jesus Christ is bodily present in the bread and wine. Not only is this not taught by Holy Scripture and our faith; it is clean contrary to that
10 teaching . . . Those wretched sacrificers [the priesthood] claim that once they have whispered or spoken over the bread and wine, these disappear, and that through Transubstantiation (such is their fondness for long and inflated words!) Jesus Christ is concealed within the accidents of the bread and wine. This is the
15 doctrine of devils and contrary to Scripture. I ask these fat monks where they have found this fine word 'Transubstantiation'.

St Paul, St Matthew, St Mark, St Luke and the ancient fathers
never speak thus; when they write of the Last Supper they refer
quite simply only to bread and wine . . . Who then will tolerate
20 such charlatans, pests and false AntiChrists? As enemies of God
and Holy Writ let them be rejected and utterly detested!

Publication of the Placards caused a somersault in the King's policy
towards religious dissent. The Protestants had plainly abandoned the
blurred middle ground of belief and had shown their faith to be
completely incompatible with Catholic teachings. They had in effect
'unmasked' themselves by espousing an extreme brand of heretical
opinion. From this point onwards, Francis was resolved to act
vigorously against them.

* Within three weeks of the Day of the Placards, all Protestant
sympathisers in Paris had been rounded up and six of their number
burnt. Simultaneously, a royal commission was sent to investigate
heresy in the provinces. On 21 January 1535, Francis joined a huge
religious procession through the streets of Paris, the centrepiece of
which was a float bearing the sacraments. After a public celebration of
the Mass, six more heretics were burnt.*

Following the Day of the Placards, the investigation and punishment
of crimes of heresy was stepped up. All cases of heresy were put outside
the jurisdiction of the church courts, which could not administer the
death-sentence, and made subject to the King's own courts. Definition
of heresy was widened by successive royal edicts to include all
discussion of the Scriptures by laymen, the distribution of religious
books without licence, and the speaking of 'all words contrary to the
Holy Catholic Faith and the Christian Religion'. Procedure in heresy
trials was altered to allow prosecution on grounds of denunciation and
the right of appeal was removed.

During the early years of Henry II's reign, religious repression was
extended yet further. In 1547 a new court was established to try heresy
cases – the *Chambre Ardente* (Burning Chamber). In the first two years
of Henry's rule some 500 heretics were sentenced by the court. In 1557
in the Edict of Compiègne, Henry laid down that all heretics should be
burnt, irrespective of their beliefs.

Despite the ruthlessness of the royal edicts, prosecutions for heresy
remained rare. By the 1550s there were perhaps as many as a million
Protestants in France. Yet in the whole of Francis I's and Henry II's
reigns, the number of individuals investigated for heretical beliefs is
unlikely to have exceeded 8000. Additionally, only about 5% of
convicted heretics were executed; the rest suffered confiscation of goods
and imprisonment. In many areas of France the local authorities were
sympathetic to dissenters and ready to shield them from prosecution.

Nevertheless, because of the possibility of punishment, many
Protestants chose to emigrate to nearby places of safety. In the German

and Swiss cities just across the French border, Protestant emigrés formed exile communities. As a Catholic writer was later to observe of one such centre:

1 Strasbourg, they called it the New Jerusalem, enjoyed a close proximity to France. This was where the hydra-headed heresy drew up its arsenal and gathered together its various forces in order to come and assail us. Here was the retreat and rendezvous
5 for Lutherans and Zwinglians under the leadership of Martin Bucer, the great enemy to Catholics. This was the receptacle for those banished from France and the host to him who has given the name to Calvinism. It was here that he constructed the
10 Talmud of the new heresy, that instrument of our ruin. In short, this was where the first French church, as they call it, was drawn up to serve as a model and pattern to those we have since seen everywhere in France.

Besides Strasbourg, exile communities were set up in Basle and in Geneva. As the description given above suggests, French Protestant exiles seeking refuge abroad were rapidly drawn to the Calvinist scheme of worship. By the 1550s there were about 10 000 French Calvinists in Geneva alone, all organised in their own churches. From Geneva, the French Protestants arranged both missionary activity in France and the distribution of religious literature there. Thus they prepared for the day when their faith might eventually triumph in the land from which they had been driven by persecution.

4 Art and Culture

In the revival of the arts both in France and elsewhere in Europe many factors played a part. The technique of printing, the influence of the Italian Renaissance and the growth of patronage all helped create the environment for artistic and literary endeavour. In France, in particular, the King's household acted as a magnet to artists and scholars, and royal patronage hastened the spread of Renaissance ideas.

The fifteenth and sixteenth centuries are marked by the spread into France of new styles deriving from the Italian peninsula. In 1443 the French artist Fouquet visited Rome and brought back techniques which subsequently earned him the reputation of being 'the first Renaissance painter north of the Alps'. It was not, however, until Charles VIII's invasion of Italy half a century later that a distinctive Renaissance art began to take root in France and to replace the Gothic style of the middle ages.

During the late fifteenth and early sixteenth centuries, Italian influence was most apparent in architecture and, in particular, in the use of heavy Milanese ornamentation. The earliest example of the new

The Château of Chambord

Stuccowork and fresco from Fontainebleau

decorative style is probably the Tower of the Minims at the royal château of Amboise, built about 1495. The most spectacular illustrations of Italian influence are, however, the châteaux of Blois and Chambord, constructed by Francis I during the first years of his reign. A Venetian observer was later to write of Chambord, 'I have seen many magnificent buildings in my life, but never one so beautiful or rich as this'. The addition of the many turrets and galleries which lend Blois and Chambord their distinction, was to have a significant effect upon French architecture. In order to accommodate the new features, the soaring vertical lines of the Gothic style had to be abandoned in favour of a horizontal design, capable of supporting heavy ornamentation.

Most of Francis I's artistic interest centred upon the château of Fontainebleau. There the King rebuilt a medieval manor house in the new Italian style. One contemporary writer (Brantôme) considered Fontainebleau 'the finest house in Christendom . . . so rich and fair a building, and so big and spacious that one might house a small world in it, and so many lovely gardens and groves and beautiful fountains, and everything pleasing and delightful'. Fontainebleau was, however, distinguished more by its contents than by its exterior, which, being built at various stages in Francis's reign, has an almost haphazard appearance about it. The château was the home of Francis I's library: a collection of about 2000 works and the nucleus of what has since become the French National Library. Fontainebleau also accommodated a cosmopolitan group of scholars and artists. Together, these made Fontainebleau, as Vasari put it, 'a kind of New Rome'.

Francis I was both a patron of the arts and a connoisseur. He employed the services of the greatest Renaissance craftsman and sculptor, Benevenuto Cellini, and – albeit briefly – of Leonardo da Vinci. Francis's patronage is most associated with the 'Fontainebleau School' and with the work of the Italian artist, Il Rosso (Giovanni Battista di Jacopo). As 'Director of Stuccoes and Paintings' at Fontainebleau, Rosso was responsible for the château's magnificent interior decoration and for its gilded galleries.

* Rosso and the circle of artists around him at Fontainebleau borrowed from Italy the techniques of Mannerist art, which they then applied wholesale to the internal decoration of the château. The distinguishing feature of Mannerist art is its rejection of the realism of the High Renaissance in favour of stylisation and of visual impact. Figures thus become elongated and forced into strained poses; unusual lighting effects are employed to catch the onlooker's attention; and fantastic figures add an air of mystery to the composition.

The distortions and tricks of Mannerist art have prompted one historian (Robert Evans) to consider it as embodying 'a turbulent disharmony . . . an expression of negativity'. If this is so, then the emergence of Mannerism in French art may be a suitable allegory of broader developments occurring within the French Renaissance monarchy of the period. Despite the new power of the French crown, there lingered a sense of profound unease. Beneath the smooth veneer of centralisation and reform, political and religious tensions were building up. These were shortly to explode into civil war. Of the flaws of French Renaissance monarchy, Mannerism may be regarded as, if not a symptom, then at least a metaphor.

Making notes on *'French Renaissance Monarchy'*

This chapter deals with the growth of royal power in France during the first half of the sixteenth century, and the obstacles to this development. It avoids a chronological format in favour of an analytical and thematic one. Whereas in the last chapter, the narrative framework made the sequence of 'facts' important, in this chapter you will need to pay special attention to the overall argument and 'plot'. The following questions and headings should help you to make notes:

1.   The growth of royal government
1.1. 'New Monarchy'
1.2. Venality and tax-farming
1.3. Centralisation
1.4. Towns and estates
1.5. The *parlements*. What other factors other than the need for cash may have encouraged the growth of administrative centralisation?
2.   Limitations on royal government
2.1. Consultation
2.2. The governors. Why did the institution of the governors pose such a potential threat to royal authority? Why should the kings of France have encouraged the development of this potentially dangerous office?
3.   Religion and heresy
3.1. The obligations of kingship
3.2. The Concordat of Bologna
3.3. The growth of heresy
3.4. The Day of the Placards
3.5. Persecution and emigration. In what ways did French Protestant emigrés pose a greater threat to French catholicism than the dissenters who remained at home?
4.   Art and Culture
4.1. Royal patronage
4.2. Mannerism. What, if anything, can mannerism tell us about conditions in the kingdom of France during the first half of the sixteenth century?

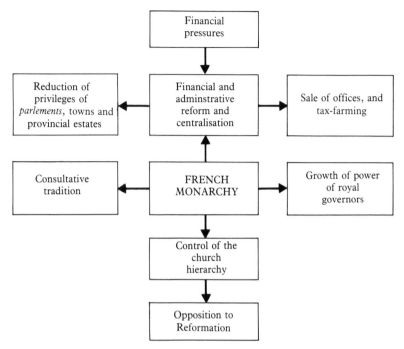

Trends in the French monarchy in the first half of the sixteenth century

---

Answering essay-questions on *'French Renaissance Monarchy'*

A-level questions on French history during the first half of the sixteenth century are likely to ask you either about the personal achievements of Francis I or about the broad political developments occurring within the kingdom at this time:

> '"A failure, but a glorious failure." Is this a fair summary of the achievements of Francis I?'

> 'How despotic was the French monarchy during the reigns of Francis I and Henry II?'

> 'With what justification has the kingdom of France in the first half of the sixteenth century been described as one of "the new monarchies" of Europe?'

In considering the achievements and failures of Francis I, you will

need to bear in mind foreign as well as domestic policy. So look back at the material you have already gathered on Francis I when in the course of noting Chapter 2. As you may recall, in dealing with the sort of terse, epigrammatic statements which usually act as quotations for comment, you should unpack their meaning as a preliminary exercise. Hence:
 - Francis failed
 - Francis was glorious
And, by implication
 - Is Francis's reign distinguished by anything other than glory and failure?
This elaboration of the quotation may serve both to clarify its meaning, and to provide you with a scheme which you can follow in planning your essay.

In any question beginning with 'How +adjective?', there is a standard approach which will always serve you well. Divide your essay into two parts, the first giving the evidence for 'Very much'; the second giving the evidence for 'Not much'. In the case of the second essay title given here, outline in what ways the monarchy of Francis I was despotic; then proceed to an analysis of the constraints on royal power, paying particular attention to the consultative principle. Sections 1 and 2 of this chapter will provide you with most of the material needed to compose this essay. But look at Chapter 1 for additional detail worthy of inclusion.

The third question will require you to give a definition of 'New Monarchy', and then to indicate in what ways sixteenth-century France fits into your model. By defining the term at the heart of the question as precisely as possible, you will provide yourself with a convenient scheme for an answer. A basic plan for this essay would be:

New Monarchy had the characteristics of (a), (b) and (c).
The kingdom of France fits this definition because it also had the characteristics of (a), (b) and (c).

In the last part of your essay, indicate the extent to which the government of France may have possessed certain additional features not normally associated with New Monarchy.

Source-based questions on *'French Renaissance Monarchy'*

1 Centralisation
Read the texts of the royal instructions issued in 1517 and 1515 and given on page 37. Answer the following questions:
a) Explain the terms *tailles*, *gabelles* and *élus*.

b) How did the instruction of 1517 threaten the principle of municipal self-government and independence?
c) In what ways did the instruction of 1515 undermine the right belonging to the provincial estates to be able to negotiate with the King how much tax their regions ought to bear?
d) What other evidence might be used to support the view that Francis I sought to reduce the power of local institutions in France?

2 The Crown and the Church
Read the royal coronation oath on page 40, and the extract taken from the Concordat of Bologna on pages 41–2. Answer the following questions:
a) On the basis of these two extracts, explain the obligations and privileges which pertained to the King in regard to the French church.
b) What advantages did the Concordat of Bologna confer upon the Pope?
c) In what ways do these two extracts explain the reluctance of the kings of France to embrace Protestantism? What other factors may have encouraged the French kings to reject the Reformation?

3 Heresy
Read the extract taken from a Placard of 1534, given on pages 43, and the description of Strasbourg on page 45. Answer the following questions:
a) What are the principal criticisms of Catholic practices made by the author of the placard? How would you describe the tone of the document?
b) What evidence is there in the second extract to suggest the author's strong opposition to the Protestant religion?
c) Explain how Francis I's reaction to the placards led to an increase in the number of those Protestant exiles as are condemned by the author of the second extract?
d) What do these two extracts tell us about the nature of religious debate in the first half of the sixteenth century?

4 Art
Look at the illustrations of the château of Chambord and of a part of the interior decoration of Fontainebleau, which are reproduced on page 46. Answer the following questions:
a) In what ways does the château of Chambord reveal the influence of Italian and Renaissance designs on French architecture?
b) What are the distinguishing features of mannerist art? In what way does the example of the stuccowork in the château of Fontainebleau conform to mannerist principles?

CHAPTER 4

The Origins of the French Wars of Religion

1 Francis II

On 30 June 1559, in the course of a tournament held to celebrate the Peace of Cateau–Cambrésis, splinters from a broken lance pierced the eye and throat of Henry II. Ten days later, the King died of his wounds, leaving behind him four small sons and a daughter. The eldest of these, the fifteen-year old Francis, was immediately proclaimed Henry's successor.

In the sixteenth century, monarchy was still understood in largely personal terms. Although the King might be shielded from the outside world by his courtiers and officials, the character and appearance of the ruler still mattered to the great lords and dignitaries who came most regularly into his presence. Despite their faults, Francis II's predecessors had acted and looked the part of royalty. Each had resembled the contemporary definition of a monarch, summed up by Erasmus as 'a celestial creature, more like a divine being than a mortal one'. Each, furthermore, had had the strength of will to stand up to critics in the court and the experience to play the leading noblemen off against each other. However, Francis II was no more than a child. Frail, both physically and mentally, he lacked all kingly qualities. In short, he was weak; therefore, under his rule the authority of the French monarchy was also weak. In the political void caused by Francis's feeble rule, hungry rivals fell upon each other and tried to grasp power for themselves.

2 The Guises and their Rivals

During Henry's reign, influence at court had been shared by two aristocratic families. The first of these, the Montmorency family, was led by the elderly Constable of France, Anne of Montmorency (Anne was a male name at this time). The second family was that of the Guises, which was headed by Duke Francis of Guise and by his brother, Cardinal Charles of Lorraine. The Guise and Montmorency families had for long been bitter adversaries and both constantly strove to out-manoeuvre the other in the struggle for dominance at court.

With the accession of Francis II, the Guises moved rapidly to secure their own position and to humble their rivals. They had an immediate advantage since their niece, the young Mary Stuart, was Francis's wife. The Duke of Guise and the Cardinal of Lorraine persuaded the king to deprive Montmorency of all his offices and to give them full control of the army, church affairs and foreign policy. Within three days of Francis's accession the English ambassador was able to report that 'the house of Guise ruleth and doth all about the French King'.

Despite Montmorency's fall from favour, the Guises still faced strong opposition from other leading noblemen at court. The Constable's three nephews, Coligny, Dandelot and Ôdet, all of whom belonged to the Châtillon family, soon began to foment their own intrigues against the Guises. The Châtillon brothers had all done well under Henry II and had benefitted from their close blood-relationship with Montmorency. Gaspard of Coligny was admiral of France, Dandelot was colonel-general of infantry and Ôdet was both a bishop and a cardinal.

The two Bourbon princes, King Anthony of Navarre and Louis of Condé, his brother, were similarly suspicious of the Guises. After the treason of Constable Bourbon in 1523, the Bourbon family had kept away from the court, since its members were held to share in the Constable's disgrace. Gradually, though, the Bourbons had rebuilt their power. In 1548 Anthony had acquired by marriage the petty kingdom of Navarre and other properties in the south-west. The Bourbon brothers had long sought to regain their old influence at court and the death of Henry II seemed a good opportunity. As 'princes of the blood' (sharing a common ancestry with the King), the Bourbons believed themselves to have a right to advise the King, and they were accordingly resentful of the Guises' preeminence.

3 Clientage

The conflict between the Guises, Châtillons and Bourbons was primarily a personal contest for power. However, two influences combined to carry the conflict beyond the confines of the court and deep into French society. The first of these influences was the system of clientage; the second, which will be considered in the next section, was religious allegiance.

The great aristocratic families of France had for long been building up power-bases of their own in the countryside. This development was greatly hastened by the creation of governorships, which allowed individual members of the great nobility to set themselves up as virtually independent rulers in parts of the kingdom. The power of the governors and of the leading aristocracy – the two being largely synonymous – was extended by the spread of clientage. During the sixteenth century, members of the French nobility increasingly turned to the various aristocratic families for pensions (cash subsidies), for employment and for protection. In return for these favours, they gave their lords or patrons political and military assistance when required. The noble clients of the great aristocratic leaders were for their part the patrons of poorer noblemen. The advantages for both lord and servant of the system of clientage, or 'bastard feudalism' as it is sometimes called, were obvious, as this contemporary account by Francis de la Noue makes clear:

1 Poverty often obliges the poorer gentry to place their children as pages, wherever they can, quite as much to get rid of the burden of their keep as to have them educated. It is notorious that there are a multitude of nobles with no more than 700 or 800 *livres*
5 yearly income who have four or five boys growing up round the family hearth. I ask you what else they can do but beg their richer neighbours to give them board and instruction. Thence arises a very strict obligation, both from father and child, to him who shows them this kindness.

As a consequence of this development, there were by the middle years of the sixteenth century, three ramified networks of clients stretching across France, each headed by one of the great aristocratic families of the realm. The Montmorency and Châtillon families, therefore, controlled much of Languedoc, Provence and Île de France; the Bourbons dominated the south-west; and the Guises were powerful in Burgundy and Champagne.

* Historians have commonly presented the system of clientage as a threat to royal government. The presence of such powerful groupings, it is argued, enfeebled the crown and placed the kingdom at the mercy of the aristocratic factions. There is, however, much to suggest that under a strong monarch the clientage networks could be used to the actual benefit of the crown. As the Venetian ambassador to the French court noted:

1 What best preserves and increases the affection of the people is their own interest and hope of something useful, for the King of France, being able to distribute so many places, offices and magistracies, so much wealth of the church, so many appoint-
5 ments, pensions and emoluments, and so many privileges and honours, which are infinite in this kingdom, divides everything among his own Frenchmen . . . For this reason there has never been a time in France when the people rebelled against their King to call another prince to the throne . . . Everyone loves, even
10 adores, his king; everyone promptly expends his goods, risks his life in the royal service, subordinates convenience to trouble, pleasure to peril, leisure to toil, in order either to make an example of himself or out of hope of reward.

In short, at the apex of the various pyramids of clients stood the King. The favours he dispensed were passed down through the aristocratic leaders to their supporters in the provinces. In this way, the clientage-networks were brought into dependence on the crown and might as such be employed to buttress royal authority. As one historian (Howell Lloyd) has observed, 'Great patrons and their clients were in the last resort [the King's] dependants; notwithstanding incidental loyalties, the complex of groups which they composed was in effect an informal hierarchy for distributing offices and favours that emanated, ultimately, from above'.

The ability of the crown to dominate and control the clientage-networks depended on the monarchy having sufficient rewards to dispense. Crucially though, by the 1550s the resources available to the crown were fast becoming exhausted. The legacy of the Habsburg–Valois wars was debt on an unprecedented scale. By the death of Henry II, the crown owed at least 12 million *livres*, of which a half was due for immediate repayment.

This calamitous situation called for drastic remedies. On assuming power in 1559, the Guises at once took charge of the treasury and insisted upon harsh measures to alleviate the royal debt. A forced loan was raised and, simultaneously, the flow of favours and pensions from the court was dammed. By December 1560 the Guises were able to boast that they had cut back on court expenditure by more than two million *livres*. There were, however, exceptions to the policy of financial retrenchment: the clients of the Guise family. Not only did they have their arrears of salary and of rewards made up, but they were also granted yet more favours from the royal purse. Unsurprisingly, there was a flight of noblemen over to the side of the Guises, anxious to become their clients. Meanwhile, the remaining clients of the Bourbon and Montmorency families began pressing their lords to break the influence of the Guises at court and to release funds for their own pockets.

4 Religion

Until the reign of Henry II, the Protestant movement in France posed little threat to the crown or to the established church. Although numerous, the Protestants were badly organised and their churches were few. Generally, French protestantism consisted only of small groups of persons who met occasionally together for prayer and religious discussions. In view of the harshness of the royal edicts against heresy, the holding of public services was considered too dangerous.

All this changed in the 1550s. The Calvinist congregations which had been gathering just beyond the border began a new offensive aimed at winning converts and at setting up their own church organisation in France. By the middle of the decade, Calvinist churches were fully constituted in Paris, Meaux, Angers and Poitiers. From these centres, missionaries were sent out and fresh converts were made. By May 1558, Jean Maçar, minister of the reformed church in Paris, was able to report to Calvin in Geneva, 'The fire is lit in all parts of this kingdom and all the waters in the sea will not suffice to extinguish it'. Nor was Maçar exaggerating; an estimate made only a few years later, in 1562, put the number of Calvinist churches at 1750, and reckoned that the new faith had a following of some two million persons, more than ten per cent of the population. Support for the reformed religion was greatest in the southern and western parts of France, and there was a particularly heavy concentration of Calvinist churches in Languedoc and along the valley of the Garonne.

During the late 1550s, and partly as a consequence of its rapid growth, the Calvinist movement in France gained increasing confidence. There were open demonstrations on the streets of Paris and congregations assembled publicly in defiance of the heresy laws. On occasions, Calvinist zeal resulted in rioting and in attacks on Catholic churches and processions. In 1559 the first Calvinist national synod met in Paris to lay down a confession of faith and to establish a uniform structure for all the reformed churches of France. As the articles drawn up by the national synod make clear, a Calvinist church hierarchy was already in existence by 1559, complete with elected offices and a regional organisation of consistories and provincial synods:

1 In those places in which Church-Order is not yet established, both Elders and Deacons shall be chosen by the common suffrage of pastors and people; but where the Discipline is already constituted, it shall be done by the Minister and Church-Council,
5 who shall give them their charge, and they shall subscribe to the Confession of Faith professed and avowed by us, then they shall be presented to the people; and in case anyone should oppose their election, it shall be debated and determined in the Consistory; but if they cannot agree, it shall be referred unto the
10 Provincial Synod.

Calvinism proved particularly attractive to the townsfolk of France. By 1560 about fifteen to twenty per cent of Rouen's population was Calvinist, and in La Rochelle, Montauban, Montpellier and Caen the number of converts probably exceeded 50%. However, it was not just in the urban centres that Calvinism won recruits. Amongst the nobility of the kingdom there was substantial growth also. Altogether by the end of the 1550s over a third of the French nobility had been won over to the new faith.

* The rapid acceptance of Calvinism by so many nobles has been variously ascribed to anticlericalism and to the influence of their womenfolk, who seem to have been attracted early on to the reformed religion. Undoubtedly though, a powerful force for conversion was the system of clientage. For there was a strong tendency for clients to follow

their lords in the matter of religious belief. Thus, for instance, in Normandy the conversion of the Count of Montgomery was rapidly followed by the conversion of five families of noble supporters. Again, in the case of the fickle Count of Lude, it has been shown that his clients changed their faith whenever the Count changed his.

The conversion of the Bourbon and Châtillon families had the greatest influence on the religious allegiance of the French nobility. In 1557 King Anthony of Navarre was won over. He proved, however, a lukewarm recruit who never shrugged off for long his habit of attending Catholic Mass. More constant was Anthony's brother, Louis of Condé, who announced his own conversion in 1558. Condé soon acquired the status of political leader of the French Calvinists, although the sincerity of his convictions were doubted by some. In the case of the Châtillon brothers, however, there can be no doubting the integrity of their beliefs. All three – Coligny, Dandelot and Cardinal Ôdet – openly professed the reformed religion and made clear their readiness to advance the new faith even at the expense of their worldly ambitions.

In contrast to the Bourbons and Châtillons, the Guises remained loyal to the Catholic faith and always professed a fierce opposition to Calvinism. It was they who during Henry II's reign had urged the King to impose the harsh provisions against heresy contained in the Edict of Compiègne. They never ceased advising Francis II to follow his father's example and to rid the kingdom of the Protestant 'plague' by introducing the Inquisition into France.

Factional politics became thus inextricably caught up with the religious struggle. The Guises, and the network of clients which looked to them for leadership, headed the party of religious reaction. The Bourbons and their followers represented the Calvinists, and they were supported by the Châtillon family and their clients who were also in favour of the reformed religion.

It would be a mistake, however, to imagine that religion only deepened the antagonism between the Guises and their rivals, and made worse the tensions already existing between the various groups of clients. For the bonds of religious allegiance extended the latent conflict beyond the aristocracy and nobility, and brought the towns and countryside into the contest as well. In those communities where the Calvinists were powerful, local leaders invariably looked to the Bourbon and Châtillon families for support and assistance. Fearful of the harsh edicts imposed by Francis I and Henry II, and now championed by the Guises, the various groups of Calvinists sought out friendly noblemen who might lend them armed help in an emergency. As a consequence of these activities, the provincial organisation of French Protestantism had by 1560 assumed a distinctly military air, with local noblemen and clients of the Bourbon and Châtillon families agreeing to act as 'protectors' of nearby congregations.

5 Economy and Society

The factional and religious conflict, described in the last three sections, was compounded by severe social and economic difficulties. By the middle years of the sixteenth century the feudal French nobility were experiencing profound hardship. Prices were rising. Although inflation amounted to only two or three percentage points a year, the nobility found it hard to increase their revenues to meet rising costs. Most of their income derived from rents, but these were usually paid at fixed sums which were difficult to increase. In addition, the nobility had been expected to participate in the Italian and Habsburg–Valois Wars at their own expense: a cost which many of their number found impossible to bear.

As the feudal nobility became increasingly impoverished and indebted, new opportunities arose for the townsfolk to buy up their lands. Around the great cities of France noble landowners were gradually replaced by merchant proprietors, many of whom gained their country properties when noble debtors defaulted on their repayments. Wealthy townsmen also purchased offices which had previously belonged to the feudal nobility, but which they could no longer afford to buy. Many of these offices conferred noble status – a point particularly resented by the *noblesse de l'épée*. As one of their number complained in a speech delivered in 1560:

 1 There are an infinite number of false nobles whose fathers and
   ancestors performed their feats of arms and deeds of chivalry by
   trading in grain, wine and drapery or managing the mills and
   estates of the lords; and yet when they come to speak of their
 5 lineage, it seems they are all descended from the royal blood,
   from Charlemagne, Pompey or Caesar.

By the middle years of the sixteenth century, the old nobility of France had begun to conceive of itself as a class under threat. Weakened economically by inflation and by debt, the nobles felt menaced by the invasion of the countryside by *bourgeois* landowners and by the proliferation of titles and offices. In fact, as it turned out, the *noblesse de l'épée* still possessed a capacity for endurance which would permit their survival until the eighteenth century. However, they were not to know this and thus for the time being many of their number demonstrated the brittle behaviour patterns and mindless extravagances associated with those who feel their social position to be under attack.

It was with the end of the Habsburg–Valois wars that the nobles first began truly to recognise their plight. No longer could they perform a chivalric function on the field, for the King could no longer afford to lead them thither. The Peace of Cateau–Cambrésis thus had as its immediate consequence the return of many disillusioned nobles to their ancestral estates in France. Some began to petition the King and aristocracy for favours, with results – or a lack of them – which we have already noted. A few resorted to brigandage. Others took it out on the peasantry, discarding old agreements and pushing up rents.

* The pressure exerted on the peasants by the returning, debt-ridden nobles came at an unfortunate time. During the first half of the sixteenth century, there had been a population explosion in the countryside. For reasons that are still unclear, the rural population had grown rapidly, expanding by roughly ten per cent every decade. By the middle of the century, France was, in the words of one contemporary, 'crammed as full as an egg'. The consequence was a new pressure on land and resources. In many regions the local economy was barely able to sustain its population and bad harvests, such as occurred in the 1550s, led to famine. On top of this, the tax burden on the peasantry had increased over the rate of inflation and by the middle of the century unrest and attacks on tax-collectors were frequent. In the dislocation and misery occasioned by the civil conflict of the late sixteenth century, peasant movements of rebellion became widespread and persistent.

6 The Tumult of Amboise

By the summer of 1559 pressure both from their clients and from the Calvinist allies was pushing the Bourbon princes into open confrontation with the Guises. The Paris Protestants in particular urged King Anthony of Navarre to attempt a military *coup* and to seize control of the court, the seat of government, by force. Navarre, although always ready to plot, baulked at violence. Increasingly, therefore, the hopes of those who wished to break the Guise stranglehold became directed at Navarre's brother, the Prince of Condé. In August 1559 Condé began discussions with other 'malcontents' about a possible palace-revolution.

The principal conspirator was Jean du Barry, Lord Renaudie. Renaudie was a Calvinist nobleman in the service of the Bourbon family. He especially loathed the Guises, whom he believed to be responsible for the execution of a relative, and he despised the *noblesse de la robe*. Thus the 500 plotters he gathered were all members of the old sword-nobility, anxious like him 'to return the government of the kingdom to its ancient and legitimate form'. Using forged letters of support, purporting to come from John Calvin, he encouraged his fellow nobles to help him capture the young King, who was at this time with the court at Amboise.

Renaudie was indiscreet, and the plot was foiled. In fighting with troops loyal to the King, Renaudie was slain and his co-conspirators put to flight. Despite its failure, the plot or 'Tumult' of Amboise, as the principal military engagement immediately preceding the outbreak of civil war, tells us much about the nature of the impending conflict. In the making of Renaudie's conspiracy lay a mixture of factional politics and religious rivalry. Furthermore, the plot relied on groups of disaffected nobles, moulded into solidarity by their commitment to the faith and their membership of a declining social élite. Politics, religion and class allegiance: the three factors were intermixed as motives in the Tumult of Amboise. It would be the same in the French Wars of Religion, where a diversity of factors contributed to the long years of struggle.

***Making notes on** 'The Origins of the French Wars of Religion'*

In the case of the French civil wars, a multiplicity of factors was responsible for the conflict. These factors overlapped with each other making them hard to distinguish in isolation. In noting this chapter, you should bear in mind that a simple or single explanation will hardly do justice to the complexity of issues which lay behind the French wars. The following headings and questions should help you make notes:
1.   Francis II. What do you understand by the statement that in the

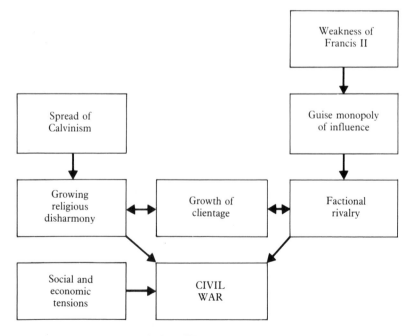

Origins of the French Religious Wars

sixteenth century 'monarchy was understood in largely personal terms'?
2. The Guises and their rivals
3. Clientage
3.1. The clientage networks
3.2. Clientage and the crown
4. Religion
4.1. The spread of Calvinism
4.2. Clientage and religion. Why did Calvinism pose such a threat to the political and religious order in France?
5. Economy and society
5.1. The plight of the nobility
5.2. The peasantry
6. The Tumult of Amboise. What does the Tumult of Amboise illustrate?

Answering essay-questions on 'The Origins of the French Wars of Religion'

The majority of questions on the origins of the French Wars of Religion are concerned with the role of religion and with how religion ranks in importance next to such other causes as the factional conflict among the great nobility.

'To what extent were the French Wars of Religion the product of religious differences?'

'Is it true to say that the French Wars of Religion were caused as much by a feuding aristocracy as by a conflict of religion?'

'"By 1559 power and religion had become inseparably linked. The fight for the one was a fight for the other." (N.M. Sutherland). Do you agree with this verdict on the crisis which led up to the French Wars of Religion?'

In the chapter you have just read, religion has been given a secondary importance. It has been argued that confessional differences extended and deepened a conflict already in existence within the court. This is, however, not the only way of approaching the problem. J.E. Neale, for instance, makes religion the starting-point of his analysis, and goes on to suggest that factional rivalry exacerbated what was essentially a conflict of Catholic *versus* Calvinist. In complete contrast, Lucien

Romier and David Parker explain the origins of the civil wars in overwhelmingly political terms. In answering the first question, you will need to establish very clearly in your own mind, and subsequently on paper, whether or not you believe the French wars to be the product of religious differences. Explain to begin with how religion contributed to the outbreak of the wars. Then indicate whether this factor was of primary significance or whether it was secondary to the factional quarrels of the aristocracy.

The third question contains a quotation from the work of a reputable historian. Do not be put off by such a device, and don't for a moment think that Dr Sutherland's opinion enjoys an authority which you dare not challenge. State first of all how the feuds of the aristocracy contributed to the ensuing conflict, then identify the role played by religion. You could in your conclusion come down firmly on one side, stating that responsibility for the outbreak of war lies definitely with the aristocracy or definitely with the issue of religion. Alternatively, you may choose to argue along with the quotation that religion and politics were so intermeshed as to be impossible to consider in isolation. To support this view, you could use the example of the Tumult of Amboise.

Source-based questions on '*The Origins of the French Wars of Religion*'

1 Clientage and the Nobility

Read the passage by Francis de la Noue on page 54, the account by the Venetian ambassador on page 54, and the nobleman's complaint on page 58. Answer the following questions.

a) According to de la Noue, what benefits did clientage bring (i) to poorer noblemen, and (ii) to those whom they chose as their lords?

b) Explain in your own words the type of favours which, according to the Venetian ambassador, the King had it in his power to dispense. What advantages did the King gain from this arrangement?

c) Explain what is meant in the nobleman's speech by 'false nobles'. Why should 'false nobles' have lied about their origins?

d) Using the evidence in these three sources, and any other evidence known to you, outline the principal changes occurring in the structure and composition of the French nobility during the first half of the sixteenth century.

e) The accounts of Venetian observers are much used by historians of this period. Why might these accounts be considered more reliable and informative than those of contemporary French writers?

2 Calvinism

Read the articles composed by the French Calvinist national synod of 1559, given on page 56. Answer the following questions:

a) On the basis of this extract, explain the organisation of the French Calvinist church in the late 1550s.

b) In what ways was the French Calvinist church 'democratic' in its organisation? How did it differ from the Catholic church in this respect?

c) How successful were French Calvinists in gaining converts to their faith? How might the organisational structure of French Calvinism have aided the process of conversion?

CHAPTER 5

Catherine de Medici and the French Wars of Religion (to 1574)

1 The Methods and Aims of Catherine de Medici

Catherine de Medici was the widow of Henry II. Born in 1519 of Florentine descent, she had married Henry in 1533. However, for most of her husband's lifetime, she had played little part in government. As her biographer (Jean Héritier) has put it, Catherine's principal obligation as Queen was to act as the 'royal broodmare', providing the King with heirs. Catherine dutifully bore Henry ten children, seven of whom survived infancy and three of whom eventually became kings of France.

Henry's death in 1559 left Catherine, as she was later to explain, 'abandoned in a kingdom utterly divided, in which there is not a soul in whom I can trust who has not got some private purpose of his own.' However, Catherine's semi-official position as Queen Mother and the maternal obligation she felt towards the new King prevented her from retiring. As a result, she was immediately ensnared in the intrigues which accompanied Francis II's accession.

As Queen Mother, Catherine was to play a vital and determining part in affairs of state. During the reigns of Francis II, Charles IX and Henry III, the government of the realm was torn by factional rivalry and the kingdom was rent by civil war. Throughout this period of intense conflict, political survival rested upon the ability to manipulate and to deceive. In the world into which she had been cast by her husband's untimely death, Catherine had either to practise these same arts or, as she saw it, give up any attempt to influence the course of events. That Catherine chose to play a part in the tumultuous politics of her sons' reigns is a measure of her personal courage; that she herself sometimes resorted to violence and subterfuge is the measure of her determination to match her opponents on equal terms.

* From the very first, critics of the Queen Mother have allowed her readiness to adopt the methods of the age to affect their estimation of her political goals. Because Catherine used the same techniques as her adversaries, it was thought that she must have been working towards the same objective: personal power. Thus as early as 1574, the Venetian Sigismondo Cavalli reviewed Catherine's career and guessed that, 'All her important actions have been regulated and guided by a very strong passion – the passion to rule.' Others drew attention to Catherine's Italian upbringing and to parallels between her behaviour and what they thought (not having read his work) was recommended by the Italian philosopher, Machiavelli. Even more, their judgement distorted

by their own religious fervour, saw evidence of a lack of principle in Catherine's refusal to back consistently one religious party against the other. 'The Queen Mother has neither fixity of ideas nor honesty of purpose', wrote Philip II of Spain; the English ambassador similarly reckoned that, 'Her own authority is as dear to her as one religion or the other'. In relying on such writings, historians have commonly presented Catherine de Medici as 'a wicked lady', whose only goals were 'comfort, safety, and personal aggrandisement' (Garrett Mattingly).

  * Thanks to the work of Dr N.M. Sutherland, a less simplistic appreciation of Catherine has emerged in more recent historical writing. Dr Sutherland argues that Catherine's main interest was a conservative one: to restore the authority and independence of the crown, and to return the kingdom to the orderly conditions which had prevailed under Francis I and Henry II. Catherine realised that religious persecution threatened to divide the state, thus weakening the crown and putting it at the mercy of the factional leaders. Furthermore, she was aware of how Philip II wished to exploit France's internal disorders in order to convert France into a client-state of Spain. These fears were, Dr Sutherland argues, translated by Catherine into a political programme. Throughout her life, Catherine unswervingly sought a formula which would, if not heal, at least paper over religious divisions. In addition, she made it her task to break the power of the Guise family. By reason of their advocacy of religious persecution and their close links with Spain, the Guises presented the gravest threat to the independence of the crown. Inevitably, Catherine's struggle with the Guises took the form of a battle for influence over the court and council, because owing to the personal weakness of the kings of France, these institutions decided and directed policy.

  However, as Dr Sutherland explains, Catherine's objectives proved unobtainable. In seeking religious reconciliation, Catherine was bound to call on the assistance of the more moderately-minded Protestant leaders. As a result, she gradually identified her cause with theirs, justifying the Guises in eventually taking up arms 'in defence of the Faith'. But once it came to actual fighting, Catherine had to distance herself from her former allies, retreating to the Catholic side. Historically, the crown was Catholic and its authority derived from its association with the established church. Furthermore, had Catherine not broken with the Protestants when it came to war, the Guises might have invited Philip II to invade France on the Catholics' behalf. Once peace returned, with the end of each phase of civil war, Catherine toiled anew to reconcile the parties and to curb Guise influence. Thus, throughout the 1560s and 1570s a pattern is evident in Catherine's behaviour and in the sequence of events: a search for reconciliation, leading to Guise hostility and war, followed once more by the quest for a settlement. Only with the complete exhaustion of Catherine's political credibility in the wake of the 1572 massacre, and her loss of influence at court following the accession of Henry III in 1574, did the circular course come to an end. It was replaced – as Catherine had always feared – by a condition of perpetual civil war, and by the march of Spanish armies on French soil.

2 Catherine and the Guises 1559–62

As we have seen, within days of Francis II's accession, the Duke of Guise and the Cardinal of Lorraine had established their sway over the young King. Under their influence, persecution was intensified and plans brought forward to introduce the Inquisition. Meanwhile the Guises' rivals were excluded from the King's presence and were deprived of many of the offices which they had held during Henry II's lifetime. So boundless seemed 'la tyrannie guisienne' that it provoked an uprising in the form of the Tumult of Amboise.

The Tumult of Amboise failed, as indeed did the succession of minor plots which followed in its train. Far from weakening the Guises' hold, the Tumult seemed at first to have accomplished the reverse. For the Guises were able to make the conspiracy an excuse for denouncing and later arresting the Protestant Prince of Condé. Nevertheless, the

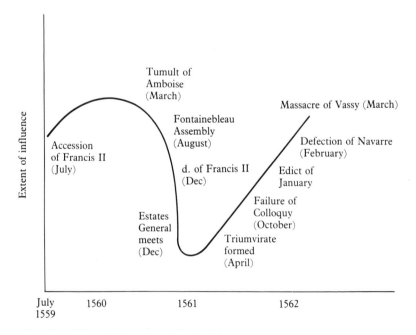

The rise, fall and recovery of Guise influence

unprecedented scale and fury of the Tumult was widely perceived as a warning signal. For the first time, criticism began to be openly voiced against the dangerous intransigence of the Guises' religious policy. The focus of opposition to the Guises was Catherine de Medici and the chancellor, L'Hôpital. Together they applied pressure on Francis, urging him to find a different solution to the country's religious problems. The success of their pleading, and the discomfiture of the Guises in the wake of the Tumult, is evident in the two measures taken by the King in the summer of 1560. To begin with, Francis published the Edict of Romorantin, which removed the death penalty for heresy. Next, the King agreed to hold an 'assembly of notables', at which the realm's internal problems might be discussed afresh and the opinion of the leading nobles canvassed.

The assembly which met at Fontainebleau in August 1560 served Catherine's purposes well. With the Constable Montmorency, the Admiral Coligny and a large number of moderate Catholic bishops in attendance, the Guises were both outnumbered and outargued. Little difficulty was therefore experienced in obtaining Francis's consent for a temporary relaxation of the heresy laws, pending a meeting of the Estates-General and a gathering or 'colloquy' of theologians. The Estates-General and colloquy, it was fondly hoped, would soon be able to discover a formula for resolving religious discord and a way of restoring order to the realm.

* By the beginning of December 1560 it was plain that the King was too ill to live much longer. Since Francis's heir was his ten-year old brother, Charles, a regency was bound to be declared on his death. Quite who would control the government in this event was, nevertheless, unclear. The factional leaders prepared, therefore, to resolve the uncertainty by force. Outside Orléans, where the young King lay dying, troops raised by the Constable Montmorency and the Duke of Guise mustered in readiness. On 5 December 1560, shortly before midnight, Francis died. That at least is known. But the precise sequence of events immediately following cannot be determined, and the surviving records do not explain how it was that Catherine managed to take power in the first hours of Charles IX's reign.

Even before formal announcement of Francis's death, Catherine had full control of the government of the kingdom. She assumed the title of regent and at once invited King Anthony of Navarre to join her in a political partnership as co-regent. Immediately, as one contemporary observed, 'everything changed'. The Guises lost their preeminence and Montmorency, Coligny and Dandelot were admitted to the royal council. Condé was freed.

The 'palace revolution' accomplished by Catherine on the death of her eldest son did not, however, solve the problems attending the government of the kingdom. The Venetian, Michele Suriano, commented:

1 As to the Queen, it is enough to say that she is a woman, but I
should add, a foreigner as well, and even more a Florentine, born
in a private family, very unequal to the grandeur of the kingdom
of France. On this account, she does not have the reputation or
5 authority which she would have, perhaps, if she had been born in
the kingdom of more illustrious blood. It cannot be denied that
she is a woman of great worth and intelligence; and if she had
greater experience in matters of state, and were a bit more firm,
she might well achieve great things. But in the time of King
10 Henry, her husband, she was held down . . . For this reason Her
Majesty has need of good advisers, but she has no one in whom
she can trust; dissension in religion and discord among the great
have made everyone suspect to her . . .
    As for the intentions of Her Majesty in matters of religion,
15 opinions differ . . . I can affirm, however, from what I have seen,
although I do not know what Her Majesty's true sentiments are,
that she does not suffer willingly these tumults in the kingdom.
And if she has not shown herself as zealous in repressing them as
one could desire, she has been restrained by fear that the necessity
20 of force would tear France to pieces . . . I know that she is trying
to hold all her sons safely in the Catholic faith and in Christian
ways of life; she speaks earnestly to this effect with many persons.
And therefore I believe one should think well of Her Majesty
rather than otherwise. If her actions do not bear out her desires,
25 the reason is perhaps that she does not have all the authority or
experience that are needed.

* As the first step in trying to heal the country's religious discord,
Catherine issued in January 1561 special instructions to the magistrates
in the kingdom. She ordered the release of all imprisoned religious
offenders and requested that no further measures be taken against
heretics for the time being. Evidently, Catherine was unaware of what
the consequences of her instruction would be. Across France the
Calvinists or *Huguenots*, as they were now known (the origin of this
name is uncertain: possibly it is a corruption of the Swiss German for
conspirator; but it may be a derivative of *Huguet*, a ghoul) came into the
open. Public services were held, Catholic churches were attacked, and
clashes between religious rivals became commonplace. The south of
France, in particular, was locked in a series of local and bloody conflicts
between Catholics and Huguenots. In order to protect themselves,
groups of Calvinist churches organised their own armed bands.
Recruits were mustered by the pastors and placed under the command
of noble captains. Elsewhere, bands of peasants took up the cause of
religion, using this as a weapon in their class-war against the nobility.
    It was against this background that the Estates-General and colloquy,
recommended earlier by the Fontainebleau assembly, eventually met.

Both gatherings were unable, however, to reach agreement on the best way of resolving the kingdom's problems. This double-failure left Catherine with the choice of either enforcing the laws against heresy or legally tolerating dissent. She chose the latter, characteristically preferring moderation to persecution. In January 1562 she published in the King's name an edict (the so-called Edict of January) which for the first time recognised the principle of religious coexistence in France.

1 We know well enough what troubles have broken out in this
  kingdom . . . and are aware of the diversity of opinions which are
  held in religious matters, of the several remedies which our
  predecessors have sought to apply . . . and of how past provisions
5 have by the disobedience, stubbornness and ill-intentions of some
  people been made difficult and dangerous to enact, resulting in
  even more persons being cruelly executed than before, to our
  great regret and displeasure . . . We for our part, having taken
  the advice of our uncle [the King of Navarre], the princes of the
10 blood, persons of our council, and a good number of the
  presidents and principal counsellors of the sovereign courts, on
  the most expedient and convenient way of meeting and ending
  these seditions, and having had all these matters well and fully
  discussed and debated in our own and our mother's presence by
15 such a great and notable gathering . . . do now ordain the
  following:
  That all those of the new religion shall following the publication
  of these presents give up the churches which they have
  appropriated . . . They shall return and restore the reliquaries
20 and ornaments of the aforesaid churches; they shall not take over
  other churches, nor seek to build any inside or outside towns; nor
  shall they trouble, disturb or impede the clergy in the collection
  and enjoyment of their revenues and tithes. We further forbid
  them pulling down crosses and statues and engaging in other
25 scandalous and seditious acts on pain of death . . .
  It is further forbidden for those of the new religion to assemble
  for religious meetings in towns whether in public or in private, by
  day or by night.
  Nevertheless, to keep our subjects in peace and concord . . .
30 we do now suspend all such laws as forbid assemblies, preaching
  and the exercise of the religion outside towns.
  We command all our judges, magistrates and other persons, of
  whatever estate, quality or condition, not to impede, molest or
  annoy in any way those of the new religion who are going to,
35 coming from, or attending assemblies outside towns . . .
  We enjoin all our subjects, regardless of religion, estate, quality
  or condition, not to hold assemblies where arms are carried and
  not to harm, reproach or provoke anyone in the matter of belief

. . . and we enjoin all our subjects to conduct their relations with
40 one another in peace and tranquillity, not carrying pistols,
pistolets, arcquebuses and other prohibited weapons, unless they
be gentlemen who normally carry daggers and swords.

As the wording of the Edict suggests, its successful implementation
depended upon the willingness of both Catholics and Huguenots to
hold aloof from violence. Since neither party was ready to do so, the
edict proved 'dead from birth' (Pasquier). Furthermore, its measures
were so radical as to separate Catherine from her former allies. The
Guises were consequently able to engineer a rapid recovery of their
influence.

★ Until the autumn of 1561 the Duke of Guise had remained at court,
vainly trying to dam the tide of moderation. Eventually, he left the
court and moved into open opposition. He rapidly built up a party of
his own, committed to preserving the Catholic faith. Even before the
Edict of January was promulgated, Guise was able to win to his side the
Marshal St André and the Constable Montmorency. Montmorency's
decision to abandon the Queen Mother largely derived from his dislike
of the measures of toleration which she proposed. The Triumvirate, as
the alliance of Guise, Montmorency and St André was known, had the
political and financial support of Philip II of Spain. As a staunch
Catholic, Philip viewed with alarm the spread of heresy in France; and
as a Habsburg he reckoned to profit from France's misfortunes.

The defection of Montmorency left the way open for the Châtillon
brothers, led by Coligny, to assume an even greater influence over the
court. The English ambassador thus noted how 'the principal management of affairs' lay in their hands, and how both Catherine and the
King of Navarre possessed only 'the show of authority'. As Coligny
urged yet further concessions, Navarre's own fears and resentments
grew. After much wavering he threw in his lot with the Triumvirate.

With Montmorency and Navarre now on their side, the Guises had
succeeded in virtually isolating Catherine entirely. As the final act in
dissolving the coalition which she had constructed against them little
more than a year before, the Duke of Guise and the Cardinal of
Lorraine wrote to demand the dismissal of Coligny and Dandelot from
the council. Catherine obliged – she had little option – and the
Châtillons left court to join up with the Prince of Condé. Condé had
never placed much store in Catherine's methods, preferring the sword
to the law. Now, as the Guises advanced on Paris, ready to take over the
government, Condé gathered his forces. The two great power-blocs
thus stood ready: Condé and the Châtillons on the one side; the Guises,
Montmorency and King Anthony of Navarre on the other. The signal
for war was given on 1 March 1562. On that day the Duke of Guise
interrupted his march to disturb a Sunday-morning Huguenot service
being held in a barn in the village of Vassy. Ignoring the terms of the

Edict of January, the Duke ordered his troops to disperse the worshippers. In the slaughter which followed, 74 Huguenots were slain.

3 The First War

Even before the Massacre of Vassy, large areas of France had become war-zones where rival bands of religious partisans and client-noblemen fought out their differences. In this respect, Vassy was just another incident. What made Vassy exceptional was the involvement of the Duke of Guise, for this was the first time a factional leader had crossed the narrow line between incitement to violence and actual participation. In response to the massacre, Condé and Coligny seized the town of Orléans. The majority of French Huguenots rallied behind them, and their religious leaders appointed Condé 'protector and defender of the Churches of France'.

The war swiftly degenerated into a series of *petites guerres*. On balance, it appears that the Catholic Triumvirate forces gained the upper hand in the fighting, for by the time peace was agreed in March 1563 the military power of the Huguenots north of the Loire had been broken. A feature of the first war, and one to reappear in later conflicts, was the readiness of both sides to summon foreign aid. Spanish and papal troops thus fought under the Triumvirate's generals, while mercenaries were sent by the Protestant German princes to help Condé. Elizabeth of England also despatched forces to help the Huguenots and these briefly seized the port of Le Havre.

At the time hostilities commenced, Catherine was with her son at Fontainebleau. The King and his mother were captured there by the Triumvirate and made to denounce the Huguenot leaders as rebels. Despite her virtual imprisonment, Catherine was still able to launch a number of peace initiatives. At first her proposals were scorned, for neither side was prepared to make concessions. A series of unforeseen events, however, intervened. In October 1562 the King of Navarre was killed by musket-fire as he laid siege to Rouen. The shot was aimed, so contemporaries tell, even as the King made a lewd gesture at Rouen's defenders. In less ignominious circumstances, at the battle of Dreux (December 1562), the Marshal St André was slain and both Condé and Montmorency captured. Two months later, the Duke of Guise was assassinated. The Cardinal of Lorraine was at this time attending the Church Council at Trent and could not take up his fallen brother's mantle. With nearly all the leaders of the rival sides dead, imprisoned or abroad, Catherine was able to present a convincing case for ending the conflict. At her suggestion, Condé and Montmorency were released by their captors to negotiate with her. The result of their discussions was the Peace of Amboise, which ended the first civil war.

* The Peace of Amboise (March 1563) placed greater restrictions on

The Massacre of Vassy, 1562

Huguenot worship than the earlier Edict of January. Whereas the 1562 decree had permitted Calvinists to hold services in the countryside, the latest provision conceived of religious freedom in more feudal terms. The Peace of Amboise laid down that:

1 All such noblemen as are barons, castellans, enjoy rights of high justice and hold fiefs, shall have liberty of conscience in their homes and they may practise the reformed religion there with their families and tenants freely and without constraint. And
5 those nobles who do not hold fiefs are extended the same right only in respect of family-members.

On those Huguenots who were not noblemen, severe limitations were imposed:

Within the jurisdiction of each bailiwick and seneschalcy [France was divided into about 90 of these administrative units], one place in the suburbs of a town shall be allowed to those of the said
10 religion . . . and nowhere else. In those towns where the said religion was exercised up to the seventh of this month, one or two places in each town will continue to be made available over and above those other places specified in each bailiwick and seneschalcy.

Since the places specified for Calvinist worship in each bailiwick and seneschalcy were usually selected for their remoteness, many Huguenots refused to stop fighting. As a result, the Peace of Amboise failed to halt religious conflict. Nor did the events of 1562–63 bring to an end the factional jostling of the aristocracy. Instead, the feuding at court persisted and continued to be linked to the cause of religion. The circumstances which had led to the first war therefore remained, to provoke further armed conflict.

4 The Second and Third Wars

With the conclusion of hostilities, Catherine at once resumed her policy of reconciliation. She thus applied pressure on local justices and officials to abide by the terms of the recent Peace of Amboise. When these proved recalcitrant, she was even ready to send in royal troops to enforce her wishes. At the same time, she did her best to appease the various factions within the court and to overcome their ruinous intrigues. As before, the gravest threat to her moderate policies lay with the Catholic Guise party. With the return of the Cardinal of Lorraine from the Council of Trent, a dangerous element reappeared in the court. The Cardinal's close links with Spain and his resentment of the few concessions given in the Peace of Amboise, made him Catherine's most powerful and persistent adversary.

The Cardinal's principal target for complaint was the Admiral Coligny, whom he blamed for his brother's murder in the previous war. Together with Henry of Guise, son of the murdered Duke Francis, Lorraine plotted Coligny's own death. Catherine vainly tried to soothe Lorraine's hatred, even to the extent of making him share accommodation with Coligny at court. When this failed, she had the King publicly exonerate Coligny for Duke Francis's murder. The Cardinal was predictably unimpressed.

Since Catherine was unable to stop the factional feuding, she turned her attention to limiting its impact outside the court. Following the death of the King of Navarre in the siege of Rouen, the Prince of Condé claimed the office of co-regent. To prevent any chance of the government falling into Condé's possession, Catherine prematurely declared the King of age in August 1563. Shortly afterwards, she led the King and court on a marathon 'progress', visiting towns and châteaux, and addressing the complaints of petitioners. The royal progress was accompanied by a series of extravagant masques and festive processions. On these occasions, the symbols of royalty were ostentatiously employed to magnify the splendour of kingship and draw loyalties back to the crown.

While Catherine was engaged in trying to rebuild the personal authority of the crown, Chancellor L'Hôpital busied himself with the reform of the administration. L'Hôpital's purpose was much the same as Catherine's. As he wrote, 'Nothing is more just and necessary, especially in monarchy, than obedience to the will and commands of the sovereign'. To this end, L'Hôpital issued a mass of instructions aimed at reducing the power of local officials and at making them accountable to the crown. Tours of inspection were ordered to ensure that magistrates performed their duties properly and large numbers of unnecessary offices were abolished. L'Hôpital laid special stress in his reforms on the idea that justice was not a sort of private possession, to be sold off to the highest bidder, but that it belonged instead to the crown and might only be exercised as a sort of trust. It was L'Hôpital's belief that the abolition of corrupt judicial practices not only raised the prestige of the monarchy, but also weakened the network of private relationships upon which the system of clientage thrived.

* Once the court had ceased its progress and become settled again, the Cardinal of Lorraine strove anew – as Catherine put it – 'to gain control by one way or another of the affairs of the kingdom'. In particular, the Cardinal sought to extend his influence through Duke Henry of Anjou, the King's younger brother and Catherine's third son. At meetings of the council, Henry was urged by the cardinal to adopt an ultra-Catholic stance and so embarrass the Queen Mother. Lorraine's manipulation of the young duke was so successful that by 1567 Catherine was obliged to go back on some of the provisions of the Peace of Amboise.

Even while Lorraine was manipulating the council into assuming a pro-Catholic stance, Catherine unwittingly compromised her own relations with the Condé–Châtillon faction. In June 1565 Catherine went to Bayonne to meet her daughter Elizabeth, who had married Philip II in 1559. Elizabeth's escort was the Spanish general, the Duke of Alva. Catherine's reason for seeing her daughter was a personal one. On Philip's behalf, however, Alva asked Catherine to join Spain in a crusade against heresy in Europe. Catherine refused this invitation. But the Huguenot leaders were convinced that Catherine had secretly fallen in with Philip's proposal and they believed her and Alva to have arranged a variety of plots against them.

In the summer of 1567 the Duke of Alva led a Spanish army along the eastern boundary of France. Alva's destination was the Netherlands where a rebellion had broken out against Spanish rule. Condé and Coligny mistook Alva's purpose and imagined that his army was about to enter France to eliminate them. To forestall this non-existent plot, troops raised by Condé and Coligny attempted to seize the court which was gathered then at Meaux. The 'Surprise of Meaux' (26 September, 1567) failed, but it provided the immediate cause of the second civil war. By reason of the evident treason of the Huguenot leaders, Catherine was obliged in this phase of the conflict to side with the Guise party, even to the extent of dismissing the moderate L'Hôpital.

★ The second civil war lasted from September 1567 until March 1568, when the Edict of Longjumeau restored the terms of the Peace of Amboise. The 'Little Peace' of Longjumeau was, as its name suggests, soon upset. For an attempt by the Cardinal of Lorraine to have Condé and Coligny killed swiftly led to a third war (September 1568 – August 1570). The main engagements of the second and third wars were the battles of St Denis (1567), at which the aged Constable Montmorency was slain, and of Jarnac (1569), where Condé was captured and murdered. The third war was ended by the Peace of St Germain. The principal feature of this peace was its recognition of four Huguenot strongholds: La Rochelle, Cognac, La Charité and Montauban. In these towns the Huguenots were allowed complete freedom of worship and their own garrisons. But in all other respects, St Germain simply repeated the earlier terms of Amboise and Longjumeau.

The second and third wars were accompanied by the massive erosion of royal authority. Even in the interludes of peace after the second and third wars, whole areas of France refused to obey the King's instructions. In the Midi, Huguenot lords took over the countryside and refused to recognise any authority. In the great Calvinist cities, local leaders established *places de sureté* which they would not surrender. The grant in the Peace of St Germain of four 'secure towns' to the Huguenots was, in this respect, no more than recognition of an existing state of affairs.

Following the pattern established in the first civil war, foreign powers entered the conflict. During the second and third wars respectively, the Protestant princes, John Casimir of the Rhineland Palatinate and Wolfgang of Zweibrücken, invaded France to help the Huguenots. In 1568 the Protestant rebels in the Netherlands, William of Orange and Louis of Nassau, joined the fighting. Also from the Netherlands came a small number of Spanish troops. Alva's fear, however, that the French civil war might spill over into the Netherlands, making the 'pacification' of these lands the harder, prevented him from sending a full army to France.

5 The Massacre of St Bartholomew

The Peace of St Germain, which ended the third civil war, was accompanied by yet another shift of influence within the court. By the last year of the war, the Guise party was increasingly discredited. The Cardinal's insistence that fighting be continued until the Huguenots were entirely vanquished, threatened to extend the war indefinitely. Beyond this, the Cardinal was eager to take France into a war with England in pursuit of his niece, Mary Stuart's claim to the English throne. Neither Henry of Anjou nor the King, who was at last beginning to exercise an independence of judgement in affairs of state, were ready to prolong hostilities, let alone escalate them. Both also resented the Cardinal's swaggering insolence and were affronted by Henry of Guise's dalliance with the princess Margaret. Once Duke Henry and King Charles lent their approval to the peace terms negotiated by their mother, Lorraine's fall was inevitable.

By 1570 nearly all the former factional leaders were either dead or disgraced. Francis of Guise and Anthony of Navarre had perished in the first war; Constable Montmorency had died in the second; Condé and Dandelot in the third; the Cardinal of Lorraine was banished to his estates. Certainly, a new generation was ready to take their place: Henry of Guise; Prince Henry of Condé and King Henry of Navarre. But with many of the old adversaries out of the way, much of the personal bitterness of the previous years had evaporated and hopes of reconciliation could once more be entertained. As a first step in resolving the outstanding differences, Catherine planned the marriage of her daughter, Margaret, to the young Bourbon prince, Henry of Navarre.

Admiral Coligny still lived, however. His very survival was an affront to the Guise family, and in particular to Duke Henry of Guise, who blamed the admiral for his father's murder. The Guises' desire for revenge had already prompted them into organising various assassination attempts. Eventually, they were to succeed, but not before Coligny had launched French foreign policy in a frightening new direction.

Coligny did not believe that the Peace of St Germain would last. In addition, he felt an obligation to his co-religionists in the Netherlands who were at that time suffering under Alva's oppressive regime. Coligny was convinced that it would be to France's advantage to wage war on Spain in the Netherlands. France's internal discords would be submerged in a campaign which would also benefit the Dutch Calvinists. Once returned to the court in 1571 Coligny unceasingly recommended his proposal. As he explained to the King, 'The cure for civil wars is to employ the warlike part of the nation upon foreign territory; for whereas other nations take up their trade again as soon as peace is made, few Frenchmen will quit off their swords once they have put them on.' Inspired by the prospect of martial glory and by the personal magnetism of the old warrior, King Charles enthusiastically embraced Coligny's scheme.

* Catherine de Medici knew only too well what the consequences of a French attack on the Netherlands would be. Philip II would retaliate by invading France. The Guise family was Philip's ally and bound to assist him in the war. The 'Netherlands Enterprise', far from being the solution to France's internal discords, would therefore renew civil war and open the way to Spanish intervention. Thus Catherine implored her son 'to keep the peace and attend to your kingdom'.

On 18 August 1572, Henry of Navarre married Margaret of Valois in Paris. The service was attended by most of the aristocracy and the streets were thronged with Huguenots who had come from the provinces to witness the ceremony. Within a few days, however, factional violence reappeared to blight the celebrations. The Admiral Coligny, returning from a council meeting, was shot and wounded in the street. Although never established as certain fact, the Guises were believed responsible.

Coligny's enthusiasm for invading the Netherlands was not dampened by the injury he had sustained. Shortly after the shooting, Catherine and the court visited him. Coligny declared that his followers were so incensed that there was no other way of controlling them except to send them into the Netherlands. In apparent confirmation of Coligny's warning, rumours of Huguenot plots and plans for revenge abounded.

The assassination attempt had at first shocked King Charles who hastened to assure Coligny both of his concern and of his determination to proceed with the Netherlands enterprise. In the remarkable transformation which then occurred, Catherine seems to have played a major role. It may be that she had had a hand in the plot on Coligny's life and feared discovery. Alternatively, the imminent departure of the war-host for the Netherlands may have made her desperate. According to one account, the Queen Mother had only shortly before (the date is uncertain) tearfully rebuked the King:

1 After all the trouble I've taken in bringing you up, preserving your crown against Catholics and Huguenots, and in sacrificing

myself for you regardless of personal danger, I would never have
thought you would treat me so badly. You hide yourself from me,
5 your mother, and heed the advice of your enemies. You cast off
my arms, which have always sought to protect you, and receive
the embraces of those who want to kill you. I know you've been
having secret talks with the Admiral and want to plunge yourself
regardlessly into a war with Spain, which will put your kingdom,
10 as well as you and me, at the mercy of the Huguenots. If I am to
be so unlucky, at least give me leave to retire to the place of my
birth, so I won't have to see all this. And allow me to take your
brother with me, who can consider himself unfortunate to have
used up his life in looking after your own. Give me time to get out
15 of the way of those foes I've made in your service: namely, the
Huguenots, who don't just want war with Spain but war and
subversion in France as well.

* On the evening of 23 August, at a meeting of the council, Catherine
repeated these complaints and added a new measure of advice. She
urged the King to kill Coligny and the Huguenot leaders that very
night, before they could launch a new war.

Catherine had evidently briefed the hand-picked number of council-
lors in attendance that evening and they added their own arguments to
Catherine's tears. Under the combined assault of reason and passion,
Charles gave in. Wearily he ordered the execution of Coligny and the
Huguenot leaders, and agreed that, since few royal troops were
available, the Paris militia should assist in the killings.

In the early hours of Sunday, 24 August, the Day of St Bartholomew,
Coligny was murdered. The account of one of the Swiss mercenary
captains who participated in the deed survives:

1 During the night the King said to his brother, the Duke of Anjou,
'Tonight I want to prove that I am King of France, for until now I
have not been King. I want to be able to count the days of my
reign from this day onwards.'
5 At about two in the morning he called for the palace guards to
await further orders . . . Upon this the Duke of Anjou took all the
Swiss and the archers with him to lead them, at about five or six
o'clock in the morning, to the Admiral's house, for the Duke of
Guise had deployed his men as if for battle.
10 The French then rushed the gates, which were defended by
eight guards, who fought them and routed them and then closed
the gates again. In the uproar one of them was killed.
The Swiss attacked the gates and beat them in with their
halberds. The Duke of Guise called on those who were fighting in
15 the lower part of the house to throw down their arms or they
would be run through.

When the Admiral's house was overrun, Moritz Grünenfelder
. . . was first into his room and he seized him, meaning to take
him prisoner. At this, Martin Koch . . . one of Anjou's men, said
20 to him, 'We are not ordered to do that'.
As the Admiral begged him to spare his old age, he thrust him
through with the pike he was holding . . .
Guise asked if the Admiral was dead and that he be thrown into
the street. As he struggled in his agony, he pushed his pike into
25 his mouth. Then he was laid on the ground apart so that he could
be recognised later.

A similar account of Coligny's death is given by a Parisian priest:

On Saturday, between ten and eleven o'clock in the evening, the
King having heard that the Huguenots were planning to cut his
throat, kill his brothers and sack the city of Paris, ordered the
30 Louvre [the royal palace] shut up and he determined to put his
enemies to death. He then sent to the captains of the quarters of
Paris to warn the people to be on their guard and to arm
themselves, and then on Sunday between three and four o'clock
in the morning, His Grace of Guise, His Grace of Aumale and
35 others went to the Admiral's house, where the aforesaid Admiral
was wounded with a boar-spear and thrown half-dead out of the
window. And the Monday afterwards, having had his head
removed, he was dragged belly-up by the little children, to the
number of two or three hundred, along the gutters of Paris.

* It seems likely that neither Charles nor his mother intended the
murder of more than a half-dozen Huguenot leaders. However, once
unleashed, the Paris militia proved uncontrollable. The populace of
Paris was strongly pro-Catholic and on a number of previous occasions
had acted with violence against the Huguenot minority. The militia
roused the Parisians from their sleep, ringing the bells of the churches.
The combined mob and militia then sought out all Huguenots present
in Paris, residents and visitors alike, slaying them on the spot. The
bloodbath continued for the next six days and the eventual number of
Protestants murdered probably exceeded 3000. Nevertheless, a good
many of the leading Huguenots still managed to escape death, either by
sneaking out of Paris, or by hiding with Catholic friends, or – as with
both Henry of Condé and Henry of Navarre – by undergoing a sudden
short-lived conversion to Catholicism.

On news of the killings, the Catholics in other French towns
organised massacres of their own. A further 10 000 persons are believed
to have perished in this second phase of slaughter. King Charles did his
best to restrain the bloodshed by issuing instructions to his governors:

The Massacre of St Bartholomew

1 . . . to have announced in every area under your charge that
everybody both in the cities and in the countryside is to remain in
peace and security in his house, not taking up arms nor giving
offence to one another on pain of death. My last edict of
5 pacification is to be maintained and to be observed with greater
care than ever before.

Charles's order probably saved the lives of the Huguenots of Dijon,
Limoges, Blois and Nantes.

Charles and Catherine recognised, however, that the St Bartholomew
Day's Massacre was bound to lead to a fourth civil war. Both sought,
therefore, to take an immediate political advantage from the killings
which would sustain them in the new round of conflict. To rally
Catholic support for the crown, Charles gave out that he had instructed
the massacre. Catherine in turn pretended that she had long planned
the murder of the Huguenot leaders and that Henry of Navarre's
marriage had given her the opportunity she wanted. Although this
deception succeeded in its purpose, from now on French Huguenots
were bound to consider Catherine and her sons as their implacable
adversaries.

6 The Effects of the Massacre

The immediate result of the massacre was a new round of civil war. In
this phase of the conflict, the Huguenots were worsted, since many of
their commanders had just been killed. The Peace of La Rochelle
(1573), which ended the fourth war, thus imposed greater limits on the
exercise of the Protestant faith. Only in four towns – La Rochelle,
Montauban, Nîmes and Sancerre – were the Huguenots allowed to
retain garrisons and the right to worship.

Predictably, in many parts of France, and especially in the south,
Huguenot leaders ignored the terms of the peace. More importantly,
they began to take radical measures to guarantee their security. Before
the massacre, the Huguenots had hoped to win religious freedom by
influencing the court and gaining royal permission to worship. As a
consequence of the massacre, the Huguenots were now no longer
willing to put their trust in the crown. As the events of 1572 had
demonstrated, the mood of the King and the government might change
overnight, rendering all previous commitments worthless. Shortly after
the Peace of La Rochelle, representatives of the Huguenot congregations
in the south of France met at Montauban and Nîmes to set up their own
political organisation. Military, financial and adminstrative authority
was taken out of the hands of the royal officials and given over to elected
councils and Huguenot noblemen. By creating what amounted to an
independent republic, the Huguenot leaders reckoned to have a better
guarantee for their security than any royal edict of toleration.

Within Huguenot intellectual circles, there appeared at this time a radical transformation of political ideology which justified the defiant stance of the Huguenot leadership. The political ideas of Hotman, Beza and Duplessis-Mornay completely rejected the older belief that kings ruled by divine right and were owed a natural obedience by their subjects. Instead, these writers claimed, royal government was a trust, given by God on behalf of the ruler's subjects, on condition that he ruled justly. If the King was unjust, then he betrayed the trust vested in him and might be overthrown. Indeed, it was even argued that the political leaders of the realm (the 'lesser magistrates') had an obligation to depose any ruler who was a tyrant.

The massacre of 1572 affected the outlook of Catholics as well as Huguenots. Many Catholics were appalled by the bloodshed and were weary of fighting. These Catholic 'malcontents' accordingly advocated a policy of accommodation in religious matters, and they championed expediency over conscience. Many of the less committed Huguenots also embraced a similar point of view. The *politique* movement, as it was known, comprised a number of different strands of thought and lacked an all-embracing organisation. Effective leadership, however, belonged to the governor of Provence, Henry Damville, the son of the Constable Montmorency. Damville rapidly came to terms with the Protestant leaders in the south, merging his own provincial administration with that organised by the Huguenots at Montauban and Nîmes.

* But perhaps one of the greatest effects of the 1572 massacre has not been so much on history as (if the two can be separated) on historians themselves. Within only a short time of the slaughter, Catherine was associated more than any other figure with its organisation. As the power behind the throne, yet not herself enjoying the privilege of kingship, Catherine was an easy target for blame. The earliest work denouncing Catherine was Henri Estienne's *Marvellous Discourse Upon the Life of Catherine de Medici* (1574), in which the alleged Machiavellianism of the Queen Mother was made responsible for the slaughter. Estienne's treatment of Catherine is typical of the publications of the day. The Queen Mother's cruelty, lust for power, and slavery to the Guises is made the cause of the massacre. In constructing their accounts of this period, historians have often relied on such tendentious works. They have, therefore, overlooked the political background which made murder necessary.

* Catherine wanted to kill the leading Huguenots not because she was naturally violent or power-mad, but because she feared war with Spain. Throughout her political lifetime, Catherine was determined to preserve the crown against France's traditional enemy, the King of Spain. Philip II had a formidable ally in the Guise family. Through the intrigues of the Dukes of Guise and the Cardinal of Lorraine, Philip sought to force the French crown into a religious policy based on persecution, even if this meant dragging the country into civil war. Catherine, for her part, was bent on reconciliation and on reducing

Guise influence. Yet in pursuing these objectives, Catherine had to tread warily. Reconciliation might only too easily be interpreted as capitulation. In this event Philip II might choose to intervene in French affairs, even to the extent of assisting the Guises militarily against the crown. Catherine's preoccupation with Spain was not irrational. On a number of occasions before 1572, Philip had demonstrated his willingness to lend armed support to the French Catholics. Spanish troops were sent to help the Triumvirate in 1562. In the second war, Alva sent Spanish forces from the Netherlands to aid the Cardinal of Lorraine. During the third war, Alva was widely known to have advised Philip to 'simplify' French domestic politics by invading the country. In 1572, not only was a part of the Spanish fleet kept at anchor off Messina, ready to attack Provence if required, but the Duke of Alva was in strength just across the border at Mons. It was, thus, logical for Catherine to presume that, were Coligny not stopped, France would be at war with Spain. Catherine had worked all her life to prevent such a calamity and was never more determined to do so than in 1572. Hence her decision to have Coligny and the chief Huguenots slaughtered. In the charged atmosphere of Catholic Paris, these murders led to greater bloodshed than Catherine intended.

In 1574 Charles IX died and was succeeded by his brother, Henry of Anjou. During Henry III's reign, Catherine played only a small part in public affairs, for unlike his brothers Henry wanted to rule without his mother's interference. By 1589, the year of her death, Catherine was an almost forgotten figure and her passing was no more mourned than that of 'a dead goat'. Her murder of Coligny and deliverance of France from a war with Spain stand, therefore, as Catherine's last important acts of state.

Making notes on 'Catherine de Medici and the French Wars of Religion'

This chapter has two different aims: to review the actions of Catherine de Medici and to provide a narrative survey of the Wars of Religion up to 1574. In your notes, you should try to avoid writing out a detailed description of everything that happened; organise your material instead around the flow-chart given on page 84, making sure you understand how the various events fit together. In considering Catherine's role, pay special attention to her motives, methods, successes and failures. The first and last sections of this chapter should help you to develop your own assessment of Catherine's political career. The following headings, questions and tasks should help you make notes:

1.   The methods and aims of Catherine de Medici
1.1. Background to 1559

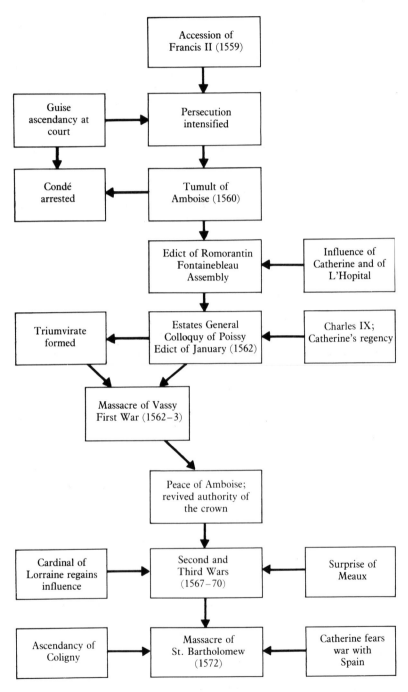

Summary of Events 1559–72

1.2. Criticisms of Catherine

1.3. Dr Sutherland's analysis

Draw up on a separate sheet a list of Catherine's aims. As you read through the following sections, write down beside each of the aims listed the methods Catherine used in trying to fulfil this objective.

2.   Catherine and the Guises 1559–62

2.1. The Results of the Tumult of Amboise

2.2. The accession of Charles IX

2.3. Toleration

2.4. The Triumvirate

Look at the 'graph' representing the fluctuations in Guise influence which is given on page 66. Construct your own graph showing the changes in Catherine's influence over the same period.

3.   The First War

3.1. Military Events

3.2. The Peace of Amboise

4.   The Second and Third Wars

4.1. The Strengthening of the crown

4.2. The Guise recovery

4.3. Military Events and the Peace of St Germain

The sequence of events between 1562 and 1570 can be confusing. List in chronological order and with dates the principal events of this period.

5.   The Massacre of St Bartholomew

5.1. Coligny's scheme

5.2. Catherine's fears

5.3. The murder of Coligny

5.4. The Massacre

How much responsibility must lie with Catherine for the St Bartholomew's Day Massacre?

6.   The Effects of the Massacre

6.1. Effects on French history

6.2. Effects on the history of Catherine de Medici

6.3. Survey of Catherine's political career.

This last section may appear to you rather too kind to Catherine. Draw up short notes on the points you would make if asked to compose a more hostile appraisal.

Answering essay questions on *Catherine de Medici*

Questions in A-level History papers often reflect the preoccupations and prejudices of a past generation of historians. In the case of Catherine de Medici, questions are still set which draw on the ideas of J.E. Neale's *The Age of Catherine de Medici* (1943). Neale wrote during the Second World War, and he was much concerned with Catherine's policy of, as he saw it, 'appeasement', which he believed to have been responsible for prolonging the French Wars. Neale's legacy is still felt in such questions as:

> '"The actions of Catherine de Medici seldom helped and more often hindered the making of peace in France". Do you agree?'

> 'To what extent was Catherine de Medici responsible for the prolonged disorder in France after 1559?'

The natural tendency in answering these questions is to give a potted history of the wars, outlining the origins of each and indicating where and how Catherine may be blamed for, or exonerated from, starting them. This narrative approach, if combined with plenty of detail and a firm conclusion, could earn a good mark. There is a strong likelihood, however, that such answers will drift into irrelevance and end up missing the point of the question.

The better approach is to divide up your answer into thematic sections. The first could deal with Catherine's *aims* and could explain that Catherine had no wish either to prolong the wars or to hinder a settlement. The second might discuss Catherine's *methods* and indicate how Catherine, by seeking to reduce Guise influence and by resorting to violence in 1572, did in fact unwittingly prolong the conflict. The third section might discuss what other factors, over which Catherine had no control, complicated the solution of France's internal conflicts.

The other most commonly-found type of question is more generously oriented in Catherine's favour:

> 'Why did Catherine de Medici find it so difficult to end the French Wars of Religion?'

> 'Why was Catherine de Medici unable to solve the religious problems of France?'

Use a 'Because' scheme to tackle both questions. Hence, for either:

- Because of the opposition of the Guises
- Because she was unable to separate politics from religion
- Because she had insufficient resources with which to impose her will.

These clauses provide you with a framework for your answer. Elaborate and explain each, using examples to back up your point of view. Do not, however, let the examples take over and swamp your argument.

Give each example in no more than two sentences. Do not write whole paragraphs on a single event such as the Massacre of Vassy or the murder of Coligny. Remember that your job is to argue a case rather than to tell a story.

Source-based questions on 'Catherine de Medici and the French Wars of Religion'

1 Catherine de Medici
Read the account of Catherine de Medici given by Michele Suriano on page 68. Answer the following questions.
a) Explain the circumstances which had brought Catherine de Medici to a prominent position of influence in the court following the death of Henry II in 1559.
b) By what personal failings does Suriano believe Catherine to be most limited as a ruler?
c) What are the principal political and religious obstacles which Suriano identifies as impeding the success of Catherine's government?
d) Taken as a whole, how biased is this author's treatment of Catherine de Medici? How may his bias be best explained?

2 Religious Pacification and Violence
Read the text of the Edict of January given on pages 69–70 and the extract from the Peace of Amboise on page 73. Look also at the picture of the Massacre of Vassy on page 72. Answer the following questions.
a) What does the Edict of January tell us about conditions in France on the eve of the Religious Wars?
b) What evidence is contained in the picture of the Massacre of Vassy to suggest that the actions being taken here were in defiance of the Edict of January? How reliable a piece of historical evidence do you imagine this picture to be?
c) In what ways might it be said that the Peace of Amboise favoured the Huguenot nobility at the expense of their co-religionists in the towns? How might this preferential treatment be explained?

3 The Massacre of St Bartholomew
Read the account of Catherine's speech given on pages 77–8, the descriptions of the massacre on pages 78–9, and the royal instruction on page 81. Look also at the picture on page 80. Answer the following questions.
a) The record of Catherine's speech to the King is given by the son of a royal councillor and adviser to the Queen Mother. The author

is normally regarded as an untrustworthy source. Is there any internal evidence in the passage to suggest its overall unreliability?

b) What parts of the two descriptions of the massacre are likely to be reliable and which the products of their authors' imaginations? Explain your answer.

c) To what extent does the royal instruction contradict the Swiss captain's account? How might this contradiction be explained?

d) Whom does the artist who painted the picture of the Massacre believe to have been largely responsible for the killings? Using your own knowledge of the massacre, comment on the accuracy of the artist's portrayal of events.

CHAPTER 6

The Wars of Religion 1574–95

1 Henry III

With the accession of Henry III in 1574, France appeared at last to have acquired a capable sovereign. Unlike his brothers, Henry was intelligent and shrewd, and he understood the need for a drastic reform of the French kingdom. In the Edict of Blois of 1579 and the *Code Henri III* of 1584, he presented radical proposals for reviving royal authority. He planned to repossess alienated estates, to eliminate financial corruption, and to suppress the large number of useless offices. In his organisation of the court, Henry revealed a similar comprehension of the forces responsible for the kingdom's decline. No sooner had he taken the throne than he dismissed from the council the aristocratic leaders left over from Charles IX's reign. In their place, he advanced a new generation of noblemen: Épernon, Joyeuse and D'Ô. These, because they owed their promotion entirely to the King, were creatures on whom he felt he could rely.

Unfortunately however, Henry lacked the moral qualities needed to restore the reputation and authority of the crown. After an energetic start to his reign, he soon drifted into indolence and lethargy. His schemes for reform seldom progressed beyond the planning stage. He chose his favourites unwisely and they only distinguished themselves by their depravity and swordplay. Instead of hunting and fighting, the traditional sports of kings, Henry preferred orgiastic excesses and empty philosophical discussions. By the early 1580s, Henry's complete inability to match the requirements of office had driven him into insanity and reduced the prestige of the crown to a dribble. In the absence of effective government, the civil wars thus ground on.

* Henry's misrule only exaggerated the self-interest of the aristocratic leaders. As the kingdom moved further into chaos, everyone seemed intent on grabbing what they could, regardless of which religious group they supported. The fifth war (1574–76) was, therefore, sparked off by the personal ambition of Henry III's younger brother, the Duke of Alençon (later of Anjou), who was ceaselessly plotting to seize the throne. The sixth war (1576–77) was in turn caused by Duke Henry of Guise's wish to enter the affairs of the kingdom as a 'third force', holding the balance between the crown and the Huguenots. The seventh war (1580) was waged by Henry of Navarre almost entirely in pursuit of the territories promised as his wife's dowry.

* In his monumental *The Wars of Religion in France* (1909), J.W. Thompson terminates his survey at 1576, seeing beyond this date no evidence of religious motives but only 'the feudal ambitions of the French nobility to acquire power at the expense of the crown'.

Nevertheless, despite all the evidence of self-interest which Thompson adduces and which has just been summarised, most historians would agree that confessional loyalty still contributed to the conflict. All the treaties ending the bouts of civil war dealt at length with the ways of solving religious discords: evidence in itself that religion still loomed large in the minds of those who negotiated the fragile periods of peace. The power of the Huguenot leaders, Condé and Navarre, rested on the huge military and financial resources of the Calvinist organisation in the Midi. In deciding policy, Condé as 'protector of the churches' and Navarre as his deputy and (after 1588) successor, regularly consulted with representatives of the Huguenot organisations. Henry of Guise and his brother, the Duke of Mayenne, similarly relied for support upon a Catholic League. In their negotiations with foreign powers, the Huguenot leaders looked abroad to England, to the Calvinist Dutch and to the Protestant princes of Germany. The Guises maintained their close links with the Papacy and with Spain.

* The death of Henry III's brother, the Duke of Alençon–Anjou in 1584, inaugurated a train of events which is explicable only in religious terms. Henry III was childless and the Duke had been his heir. Next in line to the throne was King Henry of Navarre, who after a fleeting conversion to Catholicism at the height of the 1572 massacre, had returned to the Calvinist fold. In order to forestall a Huguenot succession, Henry of Guise took urgent measures to rebuild the Catholic party and to find a candidate for the throne who was more suitable on religious grounds. In 1576 a Catholic League had been formed amongst the Catholic nobility to coordinate their struggle against the Huguenots. Henry now revived this organisation and in 1585 announced the candidature of Cardinal Bourbon, Henry of Navarre's aged Catholic uncle.

Although many nobles continued to belong to the Catholic League, support for it was greatest in the cities. Effective control of the League rapidly fell into the hands of a Parisian 'Council of Sixteen', drawn from the representatives of the city's sixteen quarters. Led by Paris, the League became increasingly radical in its outlook even to the extent of demanding Henry III's deposition. As one influential Leaguer priest explained,

1 The power to bind and unbind rests in the people and the estates, who are the perpetual guardians of sovereignty and the judges of sceptres and kingdoms, since they are the fount and origin of them. Those who have created kings – not by any necessity or
5 constraint but by their own free will – have also the right to choose from several varieties of government that which is most useful to them.

The manifesto of the Catholic League was published in 1585 and its members were sworn to the following:

1 We have all solemnly sworn and promised to use force and take
   up arms to the end that the Holy Church of God may be restored
   to its dignity and to the True and Holy Catholic religion; that the
   nobility may enjoy the perfect freedom to which they are entitled;
5 that the people may be relieved by the abolition of new taxes and
   of all new additions since the reign of Charles IX, whom God
   absolve; that the *parlements* may be left in the freedom of their
   conscience and entire liberty of judgement; and that all true
   subjects in the kingdom may be maintained in their governments,
10 places and offices.

The Catholic League was soon recognised as a formidable force in
French politics. In the Treaty of Joinville (December 1584) Philip II
agreed to fund the League in return for a promise of later assistance
against Spain's enemies. The next year Henry III capitulated entirely to
the League. In the Treaty of Nemours, which he signed with the
League, Henry revoked all edicts of toleration and agreed to join in an
attack on the Huguenots. The Treaty of Nemours was the signal for the
eighth and final 'War of Religion', which was to carry on without
intermission for a decade.

Henry III was only the League's reluctant ally and he constantly
strove to reassert his political independence. In the royal right to
appoint generals, the King saw a convenient way of regaining the
initiative. With the outbreak of war in 1585, Henry III appointed his
favourite, Joyeuse, to march against the apparently weak army of
Henry of Navarre. He ordered Henry of Guise to attack the stronger
army sent from Germany by John Casimir of the Rhineland Palatinate
to help the Huguenots. Contrary to the King's calculations, Joyeuse
was heavily defeated by Navarre at Coutras, while Henry of Guise was
victorious over the Germans at Auneau.

The King's dishonesty was so evident as to compel Henry of Guise to
seek complete control of both the royal person and the government.
Early in 1588 the leaders of the League demanded that the King dismiss
his favourites and accept Guise's advice. When the King refused,
Henry of Guise marched on Paris. In a vain attempt to prevent Guise
capturing the seat of government, Henry III ordered him to withdraw.
Guise defiantly entered the capital and was fêted in the streets. The
King then instructed his Swiss guard to remove Guise by force. In the
'Day of the Barricades' (12 May) the populace of Paris blockaded the
city and the Swiss had to retreat to their barracks. As Henry of Guise
prepared to impose his will on the humiliated King, Henry III resorted
to the last weapon left to him. Summoned to attend the King at
Chartres (23 December), Henry of Guise was stabbed to death by
guardsmen as he waited in an antechamber. Henry III, who had
listened to the grim deed from the safety of an adjoining room, breathed
his relief, 'At last I am king! No longer a prisoner and a slave!'

Henry's joy was short-lived, for the League retaliated by making war on him as well as on the Huguenots. Under a 'Council of Forty', the League took over the government of the realm and pronounced Henry deposed. Within a few months Henry III was a virtual fugitive in the camp of Henry of Navarre. On 1 August 1589, the last of the Valois kings was assassinated by a Catholic fanatic. Henry of Navarre thus became Henry IV and the first of the Bourbon line to become King of France.

2 The Collapse of Authority

Within a decade of Henry IV's accession, the civil wars were ended and a lasting peace had been secured. The achievement of the new King is all the more remarkable when considered against the background of the complete collapse of authority during the preceding period. Yet paradoxically, the weakness of the crown under the last Valois kings may have contributed to its revival under Henry IV. With the collapse of effective government in large areas of France, only the monarchy remained as a potential source of order and authority. The fact that so many people were ready to rally behind the new King may be an indication less of Henry IV's accomplishments as of the anarchic conditions which prevailed in France during the last years of civil war.

The personal weaknesses of Francis II, Charles IX and Henry III placed the burden of responsibility for the kingdom's government on the court and council. Both institutions were rent by factional and religious rivalry, and were therefore unable to compensate for the weakness of the crown. Certainly, a few individuals in the court and royal family attempted to preserve what remained of royal authority. Catherine de Medici's tour of the provinces with Charles IX (1564–66) was designed to restore the personal prestige of the crown. Chancellor L'Hôpital's reforms were similarly intended to revive the administrative authority of royal government by a thorough review of the systems of finance and justice. In the Edict of Blois (1579) and the *Code Henri III*, Henry III made some attempt to continue L'Hôpital's work. However, the persistent condition of civil war soon undid what few reforms were put into effect.

* The failure of the crown to rebuild its authority led to power being taken by institutions lower down the governmental hierarchy. The French provincial estates thus acquired a new lease of life and began to act independently in preservation of local interests. In Normandy, Brittany and Burgundy, the provincial estates refused outright to pay taxes to the crown and diverted the royal revenues to their own purposes. Elsewhere, local assemblies took over the defence of the region. In Béarn and Languedoc the estates established a partnership with the factional leaders in their localities: Henry of Navarre and Damville respectively. The towns of the realm similarly acquired a new measure of self-government, ignoring royal instructions, appointing their own officials and, whenever possible, bargaining with the King for an extension of their privileges.

Where the towns and local assemblies were unable to fill the vacuum, local noblemen stepped into the breach. By the 1570s it was common practice for nobles to gather their own bands and to wage war in pursuit of their private interests. Many of these nobles gained royal recognition of their local authority by receiving from the King the title of governor; but others simply took the rank and power to which they felt entitled. By 1572 just one diocese in Languedoc boasted some twenty-four 'governors'. As gangs of nobles attacked nearby towns and markets, disrupting the countryside with their passage, the peasantry took up arms. Peasant organisations of defence rapidly acquired the character and violence of class-movements. In 1578 'the poor people of the third estate in this devastated country of Vivarais' began a train of risings which led to the slaughter of noble families and to the burning of all written evidence of their feudal obligations. The Vivarais rising spilled eastwards across the Rhône provoking the two-year long *Chaperons-sans-cordons* ('Hats-without-strings': a reference to peasant headwear) revolt. Over the next ten years, Breton and Norman peasants rose up, while in 1593 the *Croquant* revolt carried the flame of peasant insurrection into all the western parts of the kingdom.

   * The fragmentation of authority allowed entirely new power-structures to emerge. In the 1570s an independent political organisation developed in the Midi, based upon the Calvinist churches. A network of popular assemblies and councils took over the government of the region, collecting taxes, appointing officials and administering justice. Parallel, and responsible to, this civil hierarchy was a military one led by Prince Henry of Condé and, later on, by King Henry of Navarre. Although the military, aristocratic wing became increasingly dominant in its affairs, an independent Huguenot organisation effectively controlled large areas of southern France until the end of the century. The Huguenots' defiance of royal authority was, furthermore, sanctioned in the works of Beza, Hotman and Du Plessis-Mornay, where, as we have seen, the 'rights of lesser magistrates' were clearly expounded.

   Similar 'democratic' principles underpinned the organisation of the Catholic League set up in 1584. The League's ruling body, the Council of Forty, claimed all the prerogatives and authority of the crown, even to the extent of receiving foreign ambassadors. Like the Calvinists, the leaders of the League found ample justification for their revolutionary deeds. In the Leaguer works of Rossaeus and Boucher, a justification of regicide and an endorsement of popular sovereignty may be found which exceeds the doctrines expounded in the Calvinist theories of resistance.

   * Nevertheless, even as the realm disintegrated into the anarchy of the 1580s, a transformation occurred within the works of political theorists, Catholic and Calvinist alike. Faced with the kingdom's

complete collapse, writers began urgently to recommend the revival of royal authority as the only way of restoring orderly conditions. The Catholic *politique*, John Bodin, in his *Six Books on the Commonwealth* (1576), argued that a precondition of 'the well-ordered state' was a single ruler who held 'supreme power over citizens and subjects unrestrained by law'. Even more remarkable was the conversion of Du Plessis-Mornay from advocate of resistance to champion of divine right. By 1584 Du Plessis-Mornay was convinced of the virtues of absolutist rule:

1 Never do bad subjects lack a pretext to take up arms against their
  rulers and, equally, never do rulers lack right on their side in their
  dealings with their subjects. God who created kings, God who has
  placed them above peoples, takes their cause in His hand, and is
5 Himself wounded through insults to their persons.

The writings of Bodin and Mornay are a striking illustration of the hopes now pinned by both Protestants and Catholics on a revival of royal authority.

3 The Victory of Henry IV

Although Henry of Navarre was by the laws of succession now Henry IV of France, the Catholic League refused to acknowledge him as the rightful King. The League claimed that only a Catholic could wear the crown. On this basis, the League declared Cardinal Bourbon to be Henry III's successor and gave him the title of 'Charles X'.

With the death of Henry III, about half the royal army refused to continue fighting and deserted the new King. Henry IV's forces were so depleted that he had to retreat to Normandy, whither he was pursued by the League's commander, the Duke of Mayenne. Mayenne caught up with Henry outside Dieppe and their armies met at Arques (1589). Despite being outnumbered four-to-one, Henry's army held the field. Thereafter, Henry set about driving the League army southwards, defeating Mayenne again at Ivry (1590) and laying siege to Paris.

Philip II of Spain had, ever since the League's formation, acted as its paymaster. Henry IV's military successes obliged Philip to commit himself more directly to the struggle. In 1590 he ordered a force from the Spanish Netherlands to join up with Mayenne. When this failed to turn the tide, Philip instructed the governor of the Netherlands, the Duke of Parma, to invade France on the League's behalf. In August 1590, therefore, Spain's long commitment to the Catholic side in the French civil wars reached its logical conclusion. Parma crossed the frontier and broke the siege of Paris. Before returning to the

Netherlands, his task apparently complete, Parma hoisted the flag of Spain over the capital.

The recovery of the League's fortunes did not prove lasting. With the help of English and German forces, Henry recaptured the military initiative and in 1591 laid siege to Rouen. Once more, in January 1592, Parma intervened and drove off the royal army. This time, before returning to the Netherlands, Parma left a permanent garrison in Paris.

The League's dependence on Spain, exemplified in the interventions of 1590 and 1592, became even more pronounced as the issue of the succession took a new turn. In 1590 'Charles X' died and for a time the League could find no replacement. To resolve the question of who should be Charles's successor, the League called a meeting of the Estates-General in Paris, to which only Catholics were invited. The Duke of Mayenne proposed to the assembled deputies that the crown should be given to the daughter of Philip II, the Infanta Isabella, who was related through her mother to the Valois line. He further suggested that Isabella marry Charles of Guise, his nephew and the son of the murdered Henry of Guise. Mayenne's apparent slavery to Spain and his eagerness to advance the House of Guise to sovereignty of the kingdom, appalled the deputies. They loudly rejected Mayenne's proposals, demanded a 'national candidate', but proved unable to decide whom this should be. Yet, even as the deputies hunted for an alternative to the Infanta, the dramatic news arrived in Paris that Henry of Navarre had announced his own conversion to the Catholic faith.

* Although Henry IV was the leader of the French Huguenots and held the title 'protector of the churches', he was never more than a lukewarm Calvinist. In his personal life, he carried his religious obligations lightly; in his public life he was always ready to subordinate confessional allegiance to political necessity. If Henry is to be put in any category, then the most appropriate is that of the *politique*: one of those 'who preferred the repose of the kingdom . . . to the salvation of their souls; who would rather that the kingdom remained at peace without God than at war with Him'. In this respect, Henry may be best compared with Catherine de Medici; there was little of the Coligny about him.

Henry IV was aware that the sword alone would not win him his kingdom. At the beginning of his reign, he therefore tried to draw Catholics away from the League by promising 'to maintain and to conserve the Catholic, apostolic and Roman faith in its entirety, without altering anything'. A more determined commitment than this was needed, however, to allay Catholic suspicions. Although Henry was ready to embrace the Roman religion if such would help him win his kingdom, he realised that French Catholics might regard his conversion with cynicism. Proper timing was essential, therefore, if their misgivings were to be overcome. The disarray in the League's ranks over the issue of the Infanta's succession provided Henry with the opportunity he sought. On 23 December 1593, Henry formally abjured the Protestant heresy and was solemnly received into the Catholic Church.

With the King now a Catholic the enthusiasm of his adversaries for persevering against him rapidly ebbed away. In March 1594 even the citizens of Paris were ready to receive Henry and to expel their Spanish garrison. Financial inducements served to break the resistance of what few remained of Henry's foes. Although the purchase of Mayenne and Joyeuse cost him dear, Henry reckoned he would have needed ten times as much to have defeated them in battle. As for the Huguenots, most of these retained their allegiance to the King after his conversion, reckoning him still to be the best guarantee for their survival as a sect. Thus by the time Henry declared war on Spain in 1595 he had behind him a united country. As Huguenots and Catholics alike rallied to the royal standard, the bitterness of the previous years evaporated in the common struggle against France's old adversary. The civil wars were over.

Making notes on 'The Wars of Religion 1574–95'

As you read this chapter, consider in particular the factors which caused the civil wars to be prolonged and the reasons why the wars eventually petered out in the 1590s. The following questions and headings may help you make notes:
1.   Henry III
1.1. Personal qualities and defects
1.2. Self-interest
1.3. Religious factors
1.4. Henry III and the League
To what extent was Henry III responsible for the disorder in France during his reign?
2.   The collapse of authority
2.1. The failure of reform
2.2. Estates, towns, nobles and peasants
2.3. New structures
2.4. Bodin and Mornay
Who gained the most from the collapse of royal authority in the 1580s?
3.   The Victory of Henry IV
3.1. Spain and the League
3.2. The conversion of Henry IV
Was the collapse of the League's support in the 1590s solely due to the conversion of Henry IV?

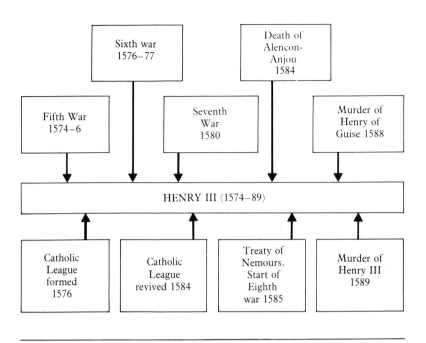

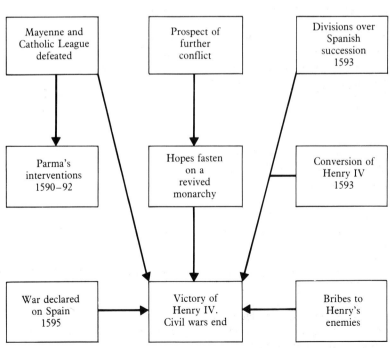

Summary of Events 1574–95

Answering essay questions on the French Wars of Religion

There are two types of question which occur with persistent regularity at A-level:

'Was religion a factor of much importance in the French Wars of Religion?'

'Why did the French Religious Wars last so long?'

These two questions will occur in a number of guises. You may be asked, for instance, whether 'religion was a mask for self-interest', or to explain why it took so long to make peace. You will need in framing your answers to pay special attention to the wording of the individual questions; there is little point therefore in memorising a set answer. Nevertheless, before attempting any such question you need to have your own ideas firmly established. Otherwise, you will waste time sorting out your thoughts when you could be writing.

In any question beginning with the interrogative 'Was?', there are three possible answers: 'Yes', 'No', and 'I cannot tell'. Let us take 'Yes' first of all. Note down all the evidence for religion being an important factor in the French Wars. Rather than write out a chronological summary, try and list your evidence under two headings: people and organisations. Which of the people who played a major part in the French Religious Wars were inspired principally by religion? How about the family of Guise? Coligny? The people of Paris? Now list which organisations owed their origin and inspiration to religion. You might put down the Calvinist 'state' in the Midi and the Catholic League. Beside each of the people and organisations you have listed, jot down at least two examples which show the influence religion had on them.

For 'No', repeat this exercise from the opposite point of view. List those people and organisations for which or for whom religion seemed to be of lesser importance: Catherine de Medici, Henry IV, Mayenne, the *politiques* and peasant movements, for instance. Again, note beside each some examples, and suggest which issues mattered more than religion.

You should now have a framework for an essay divided into two sections. The first of these marshalls the evidence for religion being a factor of much importance; the second gives the evidence to the contrary. There are two ways of finishing off. Either you can conclude by stating that on balance it would seem that religion was a factor of much/little importance. Or, as an alternative, you can attempt a variant of 'I cannot tell'. It may well be that the balance seems in your opinion to be pretty even: for some religion mattered; for others it didn't. In this case say so. But it may be that you believe religion to be so caught up with non-religious, secular factors as to be impossible to consider in isolation. The latter is a perfectly valid point of view and, although this should not sway you overmuch, is the opinion of most historians. In dealing with the question on why the wars lasted so long, a straightforward 'Because' scheme may help. Be careful to keep the content of your items broad. There is no point in writing a mammoth-list which starts with 'Because of the Tumult of Amboise' and ends with 'Because Henry IV took his time to convert'. Instead, you should build your framework around such headings as 'Because of the intransigence of the participants', 'Because of the weakness of the crown' etc. Use individual events as evidence to back up your points.

Source-based questions on 'The Wars of Religion 1574–95'

1 Theories of Authority
Read the declaration of the Catholic priest and the manifesto of the League on pages 90 and 91, and read the extract from Du Plessis-Mornay's writings on page 94. Answer the following questions.
a) Explain the terms 'estates' and 'Holy Church of God' (page 90 and 91, lines 1 and 9).
b) Contrast the views of the Catholic priest and of Mornay regarding the origins of authority.
c) In what ways might the manifesto of the League be regarded as a conservative document? Is its appearance at all deceptive?
d) How had Mornay's views concerning the nature of royal authority changed since the early 1570s? How may this change be explained?

CHAPTER 7

Henry IV

1 Introduction

Henry of Bourbon, later Henry IV of France, was born in 1553 and inherited the throne of Navarre on the death of his father nine years later. Except for a brief period in 1572, when he had adopted Catholicism to save his life, Henry remained a Protestant until his conversion in 1593. Since the Bourbon family were regarded as the preeminent aristocratic family in France, it was inevitable that Henry should have assumed leadership of the Huguenot movement. In 1588 he formally received the title 'protector of the churches of France', which gave him supreme command of the national Protestant military organisation. The next year, following the death of Henry III, he succeeded to the French throne. According to French law, no woman could inherit the crown, nor pass on to her children any claim to the throne. Although more than forty persons had a closer biological relationship to Henry III than Henry of Navarre, he alone could trace his connection to the House of Valois through a line of male forebears. Only after his conversion to Catholicism in 1593, though, did Henry gain widespread acceptance of his superior claim to the kingdom.

At the time of his succession in 1589 Henry was (as he himself later put it), 'a king without a kingdom, a husband without a wife, and a warrior without money'. The Catholic League supported by Spain controlled much of eastern France and many of the cities. The royal treasury was empty and Henry was deeply in debt. His wife, Margaret of Valois, had long been estranged from him and had even plotted against him. Yet by 1610, the year of his death, Henry was solvent and had full control of all parts of the realm. He had bridged the country's religious divisions and had brought peace. He had even remarried. In view of this remarkable transformation, it is not surprising that Henry IV should enjoy the reputation of 'the restorer of French monarchy' and that he should be regarded as one of France's greatest sovereigns.

Historians are fond of upsetting reputations. In the case of Henry IV, however, there have been no convincing works of revision or reassessment. The most historians have been able to do is to indicate that an element of caution must be exercised in assessing Henry's reign. It has been pointed out, for instance, that after the dismal progression of Francis II, Charles IX and Henry III, any ruler of even moderate competence is bound to appear notably able. Less obviously, historians have drawn attention to the way in which a legend was deliberately fostered by the King concerning his achievements, to the activities of Henry's chief minister, the Duke of Sully, and to the role of coincidence in contributing to Henry's success.

Engraving of Henry IV as 'the French Hercules'. Notice in the small cartouches *at the top, scenes of Henry's coronation (left) and of one of his military victories.*

Throughout his reign, Henry IV studiously promoted his reputation as a ruler. Artists, writers and engravers were employed by the King to develop his image as the French Jupiter, Hercules and Apollo. Every New Year different medallions were struck and circulated presenting the King in a different allegorical light: as the symbol of stability, or as the hero come fresh from the field of victory, for example. Likewise, in publications which Henry subsidised, much play was made of the new French Golden Age which the King was said to have introduced. Henry's death, at the hand of a fanatical Catholic schoolmaster in 1610, added to his lustre. With the King's murder, all his failings and omissions could be explained away as matters which he would surely have addressed had he lived longer. Within only a short time of his death, Henry had thus become Voltaire's 'blessèd of all ages', into whose reign might be read a variety of happy interpretations.

Many of the achievements of Henry's reign may be ascribed directly to the work of the Protestant nobleman, the Duke of Sully. As superintendent of the royal finances and of communications, Sully's influence affected all aspects of Henry's reign. Most importantly, Sully restored the financial independence of the crown and rebuilt the country's economic infrastructure. He was also influential in guiding Henry's religious and foreign policies. Of course, Henry was responsible for Sully's appointment and throughout his reign, he supported the Duke's work of reconstruction. Henry must thus share in Sully's glory. Nevertheless, the Duke's tenacity of purpose and intellectual sharpness made a vital contribution to the restoration of the kingdom. Without Sully, Henry's own accomplishments as a ruler must necessarily have been less.

The last decade of Henry's reign coincided with a period of economic recovery in France and Europe, and a time of relative peace in international affairs. Although Henry's own contribution to expanding his kingdom's wealth and preserving its security abroad cannot be overestimated, he was fortunate that his reign overlapped with years of prosperity and peace. His son, Louis XIII, was not to be so lucky. Furthermore, there is evidence to suggest that by 1600 French Protestantism was on the wane. As the full effects of Counter-Reformation evangelisation began to be felt in France, Calvinism lost much of its earlier attraction and potency. By the close of Henry's reign, the number of Calvinist churches in France had probably more than halved and this process of contraction was to continue in the decades that followed. The gradual elimination of religion as a cause of domestic conflict may, therefore, have less to do with Henry's personal success in bridging sectarian differences as with the declining appeal and strength of French Protestantism.

2 Religion

Despite Henry's conversion to the Catholic faith in 1593, he retained the allegiance of most of the Huguenot leaders and churchmen in France. Their loyalty derived, however, more from expediency than from affection. Henry's previous career as 'protector' of the French Calvinists made it seem likely that his attitude would be a tolerant one. Likewise, his politically-motivated attachment to the Catholic religion seemed to rule out any zealous promotion of orthodoxy on his part. Nevertheless, the Huguenots expected a more lasting assurance for their safety than the personal inclination of the King. From early on in his reign, Henry was therefore pressed to extend legal guarantees to the Huguenots which would give them the freedom both to worship unmolested and to enjoy a full share in the political life of the nation.

However, Henry drew back from granting the Huguenots all that they wanted. In his wars against the League and Spain, he needed the support of French Catholics, and he was reluctant to offend these by granting hasty concessions to the Huguenots. The Edict of Mantes (1591), which was Henry's first royal edict affecting the religious organisation of France, did not therefore extend the limits of Huguenot worship much beyond those allowed by Henry III in the 1570s. When a Huguenot assembly, meeting in 1593, asked the King to go beyond this measure, Henry rejected its plea out of hand.

Henry's apparent neglect of their interests drew many Huguenots into opposition to the crown and compelled their leaders to adopt a threatening posture. After 1594 the Huguenot political organisation in the Midi was strengthened and approaches were made to the German Elector Palatine to take over the vacant office of 'protector'. The Huguenot national assembly was also summoned to consider matters of defence. By 1597 this body was in permanent session and was recommending Huguenots not to pay taxes to the King. Meanwhile, the aristocratic champions of the Huguenot religion withdrew their support from the monarch. Even as Henry battled with the Spanish forces outside Amiens, the Protestant Duke of Bouillon refused to lend military support to the King and opened up negotiations with the enemy.

By 1598 Henry was ready to parley with the Huguenots. His hand in the negotiations which followed was greatly strengthened by the recent defeat of Spain which freed the royal armies for deployment against the Huguenots should they prove stubborn in discussions. Nevertheless, it was only after much hard bargaining that the settlement known as the Edict of Nantes (1598) was finally reached.

* The Edict of Nantes consisted of four separate treaties: 92 general articles, 56 explanatory schedules and two royal letters (*brevets*). Although the Huguenots were granted complete liberty of conscience, substantial restrictions still applied to public worship. Protestant congregations might meet unhindered on the estates of Huguenot noblemen, in two places in each bailiwick, and in all those places where they had been worshipping publicly in 1597. Because the provisions affecting the bailiwicks proved unenforceable in Catholic areas, the practice of Huguenot worship was largely confined to the western and southern parts of France. The Huguenots were additionally permitted 50 garrisons paid for by the crown, 80 forts and 150 other 'places of refuge', the majority of which were similarly restricted in their location. Huguenots were also allowed to hold offices of the crown and were permitted to have legal cases affecting them heard by mixed benches (*chambres mi-parties*) of Huguenot and Catholic judges.

Historians have often charged that the Edict of Nantes established 'a state within the state' or, in other words, an independent Huguenot organisation which functioned quite separately from the rest of France. This cannot be the case. First, Huguenots were still bound to follow the laws of the land; they were not empowered to set up their own courts but had instead to prosecute cases before royal judges. Secondly, discussion of all political matters was denied to the Huguenot national and provincial assemblies, and royal officers were entitled to attend the religious discussions of these bodies. Finally, Huguenots still had to obey the King and, for refusal to do so, might be indicted on charges of treason.

At most, the Edict of Nantes created a new 'estate': a group of persons holding special privileges. However, the Huguenot 'estate' lacked many of the characteristics of the other, more established estates of the realm such as the clergy and nobility. The Huguenots neither enjoyed corporate representation nor possessed any special constitutional prerogatives. They did not, therefore, meet as a separate chamber either in the Estates-General or in the provincial estates. Nor was the privileged position of the Huguenots buttressed by any long historical tradition. Their status was of recent creation and it depended solely upon a decree of the crown. And because it was no more than an expression of royal favour, the Edict of Nantes could be revoked at the King's pleasure. Indeed, the almost temporary character of the Edict is apparent in the fact that many of its terms were published in the form of royal *brevets*, letters which became automatically invalid on the sovereign's death.

Far from creating 'a state within the state', the Edict of Nantes only confirmed the Huguenots' dependence on the monarch. In this respect, the Huguenots were fortunate that Henry never withdrew his concessions, but endeavoured instead to set an example of toleration and of even-handedness. In his personal appointments, the King took care to show equal favour to Huguenots and Catholics; in the bestowal of patronage he was impartial. Those who failed to match the King's example were treated roughly by him, as the leading townsmen of Toulouse were soon to find. In 1599 Henry addressed them as follows:

1 It is strange that you cannot cast out your ill will. I see that you still have Spanish notions in your bellies. Who, then, can believe that those who have exposed their life, property and honour for the defence and preservation of this state are not worthy of
5 honourable public posts in it? . . . But those who have done their very best to wreck the state are to be seen as good Frenchmen, worthy of such posts! I am not blind; I see through all this, and wish that those of the Religion should be able to live at peace in my realm and be eligible for all posts, not because they are
10 Protestants, but because they have faithfully served me and the French crown. I wish to be obeyed, and that my edict shall be published and implemented throughout my kingdom. It is high time that all of us, drunk with war, sobered up.

As a consequence of the pattern of impartiality established and enforced by the King, disaffected Huguenot noblemen were never able to rally behind them more than a handful of religious malcontents. In short, therefore, if the Edict of Nantes 'settled' the religious affairs of France, it did so only because the King continued to wish this to be so. And when the King no longer saw fit to tolerate the Huguenot religion, as happened with Louis XIV in 1685, persecution would return in its full severity.

3 Finance and Administration

The financial position which Henry IV inherited was desperate. The crown's annual expenditure exceeded income by 18 million *livres* and its debts amounted to 200 million *livres*. Since royal income was barely 30 million *livres* there seemed little possibility of ever balancing the budget. Indeed, the war with Spain and Henry's policy of buying off his enemies with bribes threatened to extend the imbalance yet further. Nor did the fiscal administration seem at all capable of rising to the challenge of meeting the King's needs. Many financial offices had been sold off and large parts of the royal revenues had been mortgaged. Elsewhere, the system of taxation had been taken over by hostile forces; as late as 1596 it was reckoned that one-fifth of the royal income was being diverted into the coffers of Henry's enemies. Thus, throughout the 1590s, Henry had to adopt the clumsy expedient of using whatever he had at hand to pay for the needs of the moment. Since necessity far outweighed cash, policy floundered on the shoals of insolvency. The army was regularly left unpaid and mutinous, and angry creditors attacked royal officials, demanding payment. Henry himself was obliged to trim his personal expenditure to an extent which even he, no stranger to hardship, found intolerable. As he wrote in 1596, 'My shirts are torn, my trousers are worn out, my larder is bare, and for two days I have had to dine with others. My catering staff say that they can no longer feed me because they have received no money for the past six months.'

In 1596 Henry summoned an assembly of notables to discuss a remedy for the financial crisis. The gathered nobles and officials soon fell to quarrelling amongst themselves as each sought to justify his own past handling of royal monies and to cast doubts on the competence of his colleagues. The English ambassador, who attended the assembly as an observer, wrote:

1 The assembly of our deputies here hath not yet brought forth anything in perfect shape, but only affordeth matters of discourse and expectation, and every day more and more discovereth the disagreeing humours, factions and poverty of this state, some
5 seeking to defend their own faults by way of a diversion upon

others, many practising to dissolve the assembly, and all labouring to make this reformation serve their own terms.

After much bickering, the assembly agreed to the King's suggestion of a 5% sales tax on all transactions. However, the edict establishing this new imposition was long held up in the Paris *parlement* and actual collection of the *pancarte* – as the tax was known – only began in 1601. Furious resistance to the *pancarte* in the towns, and uprisings in Poitiers and La Rochelle, obliged Henry to agree to its abolition the next year.

  * The 1596 assembly and the fate of the *pancarte* amply illustrate the obstacles to financial reform with which Henry had to contend. Agreement to new taxes was hard to reach; innovation was resented; and implementation was resisted. These limitations on financial reconstruction were well understood by the Duke of Sully, who became superintendent of the royal finances in 1598. Sully's greatest achievement was to transform the royal finances from a condition of paralysis and debt to one of solvency by the end of Henry's reign. By 1610 not only was current income running well above expenditure, but 16 million *livres* were at hand in ready cash in the royal treasuries. In accomplishing this remarkable transformation, Sully largely avoided innovation and relied on traditional methods of raising revenue.

  On being appointed superintendent in 1598, Sully began the immediate investigation of the royal fiscal administration. His enquiries were detailed and thorough. In his autobiography, Sully applauded the diligence with which he applied himself to this task:

1 You [Sully: he addressed his memoirs to himself] forthwith (as was your custom) pursued all sorts of enquiries in the registers of the Council of State, the *parlements*, the *chambres des comptes, cour des aides* as well as from former secretaries of state (for those in
5 office would reveal nothing), colleges of treasurers, treasurers at the exchequer and treasury, and in the book of ordinances, from which you made copies and drew up instructions and memoranda on state policy relating to finance so as to be able to administer this area with such rules and regulations . . . that the revenues of
10 France might be restored to their proper value, and royal taxes so well managed and accounted for that there would no longer be any misappropriation. In this, you laboured with assiduous care, day and night . . .

In his review of the financial system, Sully was much helped by the survival of the apparatus for tax collection, despite the decades of civil war. The local warlords and military organisations which had dominated the provinces during the fighting had seldom abolished the machinery of taxation in those areas under their control. Instead, they had preserved what they found, diverting the money raised to serve their own ends. Once order had returned to the kingdom, the crown was able to resume control with little difficulty. In order to reimpose discipline and uniformity on the lower echelons of the financial administration, Sully kept up a constant flow of orders and instructions. Treasury officials who proved slack or corrupt were dismissed. Those financiers who had bought the right to collect taxes in certain parts of the kingdom, were subjected to special judicial enquiries and made to repay any money they had embezzled.

The royal debts were, however, so enormous as to remain virtually unaffected by such improvements. Sully's solution to this problem was straightforward. He simply informed those to whom Henry owed money that the King was penniless and that they would have to make do with a part-payment. The governments of England, of the United Provinces, and of the individual Swiss cantons, from all of which Henry had borrowed, resented Sully's methods but were powerless to extract their full due. Similarly unscrupulous tactics were employed against Frenchmen who had lent to the crown. Many were refused payment outright, others had to put up with only a portion. The interest payable on bonds or *rentes* (securities sold by the crown in return for an annual payment) was reduced and some bonds were declared invalid. The devices used by Sully to discharge the royal debt may seem crude and unfair. Sully's instructions from the king were, however, clear: 'to increase the revenue and not to deliver justice'. Sully fulfilled this prescription exactly.

Sully's most enduring achievement was to shift the burden of taxation from the Third Estate to the privileged orders. During his term of office, the *taille* actually dropped as measures were applied to ensure its more equal distribution. The shortfall in the *taille* was made up for by raising the *gabelle*, the tax paid on salt by nobles and non-nobles alike. Furthermore, because the value of the *gabelle* related immediately to the price of salt, the *gabelle* did not decline in real terms as a result of inflation.

★ The *gabelle* was far outstripped in value by the ingenious tax first raised by Sully in 1604 and called the *paulette*. Named after its inventor, the financier Charles Paulet, the *paulette* was a tax on the class of office-holders which had risen to power and influence during the sixteenth century. By Henry's reign, it was plain that the device of creating and selling offices in return for an annual pension or the right to collect a certain revenue, was no solution except to the most pressing, short-term needs. The cost of salaries alone was reckoned in 1596 at 2.5 million *livres*, and this figure left out the sums which office-holders might extract at source in the form of taxes, fines and commissions. The *paulette* was designed to make up for this loss by imposing a tax which was calculated at one-sixtieth of each office's assessed value. By this new measure Sully ensured a regular flow of income which would offset the cost of pensions and salaries. As a concession, Sully declared that payment of the *paulette* would entitle office-holders to bequeath their offices on whomsoever they chose.

The *paulette* was in many ways a fraudulent device. The value of offices was frequently over-assessed and as a consequence many office-holders paid more in tax to the crown than they received as salary. However, most considered the rank which they held to be sufficient compensation, for office gave status and the right to membership of the nobility. By coupling the *paulette* to inheritance, Sully additionally appealed to the sentiments of office-holders, who were anxious to see the fruits of their worldly success passed on to their children. In this respect, the *paulette* struck a skilful balance between the monetary needs of the crown and the ambitions of the class of office-holders.

By making offices hereditary on payment of the *paulette*, Sully dealt a severe blow to the system of noble clientage in France. Previously the aristocratic leaders had enjoyed a powerful influence over appointments. Some, indeed, had had huge numbers of offices at their disposal with which they might reward their followers. With the advent of the *paulette*, offices ceased to be commodities which might be traded privately in exchange for political support. Instead, they became demonstrable tokens of the King's authority, for they might only be retained on payment of an annual sum to the treasury. In this way, the *paulette* served to strengthen royal prestige and to erode the networks of private patronage. It seems probable that Sully foresaw this consequence and that he welcomed it. For, as we will see, throughout the term of his appointment, Sully consistently strove to break the power of vested interests and to subordinate all local agencies of influence to the authority of the crown.

* The regional assemblies which met in the border provinces of the realm possessed an infinite capacity to withhold taxes and to obstruct the progress of reform. Under Sully's direction, the powers of the local estates of Guyenne and of the newly-acquired provinces of Bresse, Bugey and Gex (see page 114) were reduced and their powers over taxation given over to royally-appointed officials. Sully similarly trespassed upon the rights of the estates of Normandy, Burgundy, Dauphiné, Languedoc and Provence, although it was not until the reign of Louis XIII that these bodies were finally dissolved. Likewise, municipal councils which proved obstructive had their privileges withdrawn and were made subject to royal supervision. Additionally, commissioners were appointed at Sully's direction and given wide financial and administrative powers. Acting as roving emissaries, the commissioners checked up on the activities of military governors, local estates and town councils. In the institution of Henry IV's commissioners, many historians have seen the origin of the *intendants* used with such effect later on by Richelieu and Louis XIV.

The constitutional status of the *parlements* was so entrenched as to defy all royal attempts to remove their privileges. In his dealings with the *parlements*, Henry had to rely largely upon techniques of personal persuasion. This is no better illustrated than in Henry's speech to the leading *parlementaires*, which he delivered in 1599 upon the occasion of the Paris *parlement*'s refusal to register the Edict of Nantes:

1 You see me in my study, where I have come to speak to you not in my royal garb or with sword and cloak, like my predecessors, nor like a prince speaking to foreign ambassadors, but like the father of a family speaking informally to his children. What I want to say
5 is that I wish you to verify the edict granted to the Protestants. What I have done is for the sake of peace; I have established it outside my kingdom and now wish to ensure it inside. You ought to obey me if only because of my position, and the obligation which is shared by my subjects and particularly by you of my
10 *parlement*.

I have restored some of the homes from which they had been banished, and have restored faith to others who had lost it. If obedience was due to my predecessors, still more is it due to me, because I have restored the state, God having chosen to establish
15 me in the kingdom which is mine both by inheritance and by acquisition. The members of my *parlement* would not be in their seats without me; I do not want to boast, but I wish to insist that I myself have set you an example.

I know that there are intrigues in the *parlement*, and that
20 seditious preachers have been stirred up, but I shall attend to that without your help. That is what led to the barricades and eventually to the assassination of the late King. I shall see to all that, cutting all factions and seditious preaching off at the root
. . . I have stormed plenty of town walls and shall surely storm
25 barricades too, if necessary. Do not speak to me of the Catholic religion; I love it better than you; I am more Catholic than you; I am the eldest son of the Church, which none of you is or can be. You are deceiving yourselves if you think you are well in with the Pope; I am better in than you, and if I wish shall have you all
30 declared heretics for disobeying me.

I am better informed than you; whatever happens, I know what each of you will say. I know what is in your houses, I know what you are doing and everything that you say, for I have a little devil who reveals all to me . . . I am now King, and speak as King. I
35 wish to be obeyed. The men of the law are indeed my right arm, but if the right arm becomes gangrenous, then the left must cut it off . . .

Yield up to my entreaties what you would not have given up by threats, for you will have none from me. Do what I require of you
40 at once, I beg you; you will be doing it not only for me, but for the sake of peace.

The reign of Henry IV foreshadowed the royal absolutism of his grandson, Louis XIV. Under Henry's direction, the prestige of the crown was restored, its financial basis was secured, and new steps were taken to reduce the power of rival constitutional bodies within the state. In analysing this development, it may be tempting to identify the administrative work and techniques of the Duke of Sully as being of paramount importance. Nevertheless, as the speech given above suggests, the authority of the crown owed much to the personality and character of the ruler. The vigour of Henry's words and his convincing combination of threat and plea obliged the *parlement* rapidly to give in to his demands. Throughout his reign Henry replied to similar obstruction with the same tireless insistence on obedience: 'I have made an edict and I wish it to be kept', 'I wish to be obeyed'. In the making of French absolutism, the constant repetition of such commands proved as persuasive an instrument as any bureaucratic instruction issued by the Duke of Sully.

4 Economy and Society

The long period of civil war had severely dislocated the economy of France. Manufacturing had declined and the country become flooded with Dutch and English imports. The plight of the peasantry had greatly worsened as a result of pillage and of the frequent disruption of the harvest. The establishment of private mints by ambitious local leaders had introduced a flood of debased coinage into circulation, thus adding to inflation and damaging commerce.

The establishment of peaceful conditions removed many of the causes of economic distress and helped to restore French agriculture and commerce. With hostilities over, the peasant could return to the plough and the merchant to his trade. A succession of bumper harvests aided recovery by increasing peasant profits and cutting the price of bread. Thus when Thomas Coryat, an English traveller, journeyed through France in 1608 he could find only one village 'exceedingly ransacked and ruinated by means of the civil war'. In the towns, a recovery in manufacturing took place and new centres of commercial prosperity developed along the Atlantic coastline at La Rochelle, Brest and St Malo. Nevertheless, such achievements as these cannot only be considered the consequence of a return to peaceful and orderly conditions. Under Henry's direction, the reconstruction of the French economy was actively promoted and hastened by a succession of interventionist measures which benefited trade and agriculture.

  * It had been common practice throughout the middle ages for the kings of France to regulate aspects of the economy: the operation of guilds or the price of basic foodstuffs, for instance. During the late sixteenth century, however, a greater and more scientific economic awareness began to influence royal policy. In particular, an early form of 'mercantilist' theory emerged, which argued that the best way to

increase national wealth was for the government to expand exports while simultaneously encouraging self-sufficiency at home.

Henry IV accepted many of the mercantilist prescriptions for economic recovery. He showed a keen interest in developing French agriculture, keeping on display in the Louvre a permanent exhibition of mechanical implements, and subsidising the publication of farming manuals. He was also an enthusiastic supporter of new commercial ventures. Henry, however, delegated most of the task of economic reform and stimulation to the Duke of Sully.

In 1599 Sully was appointed to the newly-created post of *grand voyer* or superintendent of communications, and it was in this capacity that he began the revitalisation of the country's economic infrastructure. The appalling condition of the French road-system severely hampered commercial development. Indeed, when Sully took over as *grand voyer*, it was swifter to travel from the north to the west of France by sea than by carriage. Tariffs and local customs barriers added to the problem of transportation by as much as quadrupling the price of articles which had to be conveyed overland. Between 1599 and 1610 Sully increased the annual royal expenditure on internal communications from 6000 to over one million *livres*. New bridges were built, roads were made passable, and although this was not completed until 1642, the construction was begun of a canal linking the Seine to the Loire. Many local tolls were abolished, thus making long-distance trade more profitable.

Sully's most ambitious instrument for promoting industrial growth was the Council of Commerce which he established in 1602. Over the next ten years the council met on some 150 occasions, discussing and putting into effect measures for increasing and defending manufacturing output. The Council raised tariffs against imports and removed all the dues previously payable on goods destined for export. Under the Council's direction, the silk-worm was introduced into France to reduce dependence upon Italian imports, and the famous tapestry-works at Gobelins was founded. Similarly, the Council provided business advice and financial assistance to the many noble and bourgeois entrepreneurs anxious to take advantage of the country's economic recovery.

However, not all the Council's projects were successful. The French East India Company, set up in 1604, was able neither to overcome ferocious Dutch competition nor to open up the passage to the Far East which was reputed to lie north of Russia. The New France Company, founded to settle and develop Canada, proved longer lasting but scarcely more profitable.

5 Foreign Policy

Throughout the sixteenth century, the rulers of France had seen the Habsburgs and Spain as the principal challenge to the kingdom's security. Francis I, Henry II and Catherine de Medici had therefore conducted their foreign policy on the assumption that Charles V and Philip II of Spain were their main adversaries. With the benefit of hindsight we may conclude that by the end of the century Spain was already a declining force in European affairs. This, however, was not apparent at the time. Spanish garrisons still held the Pyrenees and Flanders; Luxembourg, Lorraine, Franche Comté and Savoy remained in the Spanish orbit; and a network of alliances and special relationships bound the principalities of northern Italy to Madrid. Furthermore, during the 1590s Spanish troops were actually fighting on French soil, ostensibly in support of the Catholic League, but really in pursuit of territorial gain and of influence in the kingdom's domestic affairs.

In the mid-eighteenth century a collection of documents was published which purported to show that Henry IV's foreign policy was built around a 'Grand Design'. Extracts were culled from the writings of the Duke of Sully and were slotted together in such a way as to suggest that Henry's diplomatic dealings concealed a hidden purpose. According to the Grand Design, Henry wanted to redraw the whole map of Europe from the Mediterranean to the Urals, to establish a 'Council of Europe' so as to coordinate the continent's affairs, and to lead an international campaign against the Turks. Appealing though it may be to think of Henry IV as a sort of crusading Napoleon, the Grand Design was most probably not the King's fantasy but that of later writers. For in all respects, Henry's foreign policy followed the traditions of his Valois predecessors and was directed almost entirely at counteracting Spanish ambitions.

  * Two important considerations limited the King's freedom of action in foreign affairs. The first was financial. Henry IV knew his resources were unequal to a prolonged struggle with Spain and that his objectives would therefore have to be met largely by peaceful means. Secondly, the Catholic powers of Europe were wary of Henry and distrusted his motives. As a former Huguenot he was often believed to nurture a wish to lead a Protestant coalition against the champion of Catholic Christendom, the King of Spain. Henry had thus to tread warily lest in confronting Spain he should prompt the formation of a hostile Catholic alliance.

  * Henry's financial plight was never worse than in the early years of his reign; nor was the possibility of Spain mustering international support against him ever greater than in the immediate wake of his conversion to Rome. It therefore seems incredible that in 1595 Henry should have declared war on Philip II. As it turned out, Henry was victorious and in the peace of Vervins (1598), Philip II returned to France all the frontier possessions which he had seized since 1559. Nevertheless, this happy outcome was far from inevitable and the Spanish forces enjoyed some early successes in the fighting. There are, of course, obvious explanations for Henry's decision to make open war

on Spain even at this perilous juncture. A 'patriotic war' might heal the kingdom's internal divisions; conflict with Spain would be a sop to those Huguenots who were offended by the King's new religion; Spanish troops were in any case aiding the remnants of the League in France. Nevertheless, whatever Henry's motives for deciding on war, the long uncertainty of its outcome convincingly spelled out why he must in future hold back from open confrontation. The chances of a humiliating defeat were simply far too great.

   * After 1598 Henry endeavoured to construct a series of foreign alliances which would serve both to counteract Spain's influence in European affairs and to provide him with a body of international support should war be resumed. The United Provinces and the Protestant princes of Germany were natural allies, for they were also fearful of Spanish ambitions. In the Empire, Henry paid particular attention to the principalities which lay along the Lower Rhine, since this troubled part of Germany lay close to France. In 1599 he guaranteed the security of the strategically-important duchy of Jülich-Cleves in concert with the Elector Palatine (see map, page 114).

   In 1602 one of Henry's ambassadors remarked, 'Italy is bound from head to foot to Madrid . . . All has been lost to Spain'. The lack of French influence in the peninsula had of course been apparent since the reign of Francis I. France's long period of civil war had rendered impossible any resurgence of diplomatic activity in Italy, and had allowed Spain to consolidate her influence there virtually unchallenged. The strong Spanish influence in north Italy was particularly threatening. The duchy of Milan was the assembly-point for Spanish troops bound for the long march to the Netherlands along the 'Spanish Road'. From Milan and from points along the Spanish Road the King of Spain could easily launch an invasion-force into France.

   Henry worked hard to rebuild French power in the peninsula. In 1600 Henry married Marie de Medici, the niece of the Grand Duke of Tuscany, thus providing himself with a wealthy and powerful ally in Italy. By helping Pope Clement VIII to annex Ferrara, and by re-admitting the Jesuits into France in 1603, Henry won the friendship of the Papacy. When a few years later, the Pope fell out with the ruling council of the Venetian republic, Henry offered to mediate in the quarrel. Because he managed to settle the dispute amicably, he simultaneously increased his standing with Rome and secured the friendship of Venice. Venice's support proved a welcome gain, for the republic controlled the Valtelline passes of the Alps through which one of the routes of the Spanish Road led. Further to the west, Henry rebuilt the old French alliance with the Swiss confederation and applied a formidable military pressure on Spain's ally, the Duke of Savoy. After a brief war in 1600–1, the Duke of Savoy was compelled to exchange his alliance with Spain for one with France, and to give over to Henry the provinces of Bresse, Bugey and Gex, which straddled the Spanish

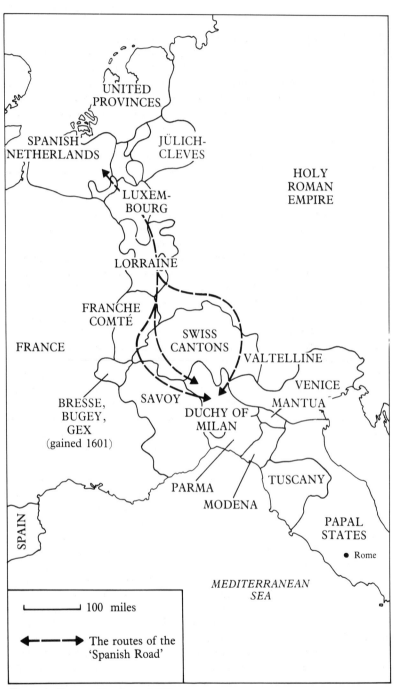

UNITED
PROVINCES

SPANISH
NETHERLANDS

JÜLICH-
CLEVES

HOLY
ROMAN
EMPIRE

LUXEM-
BOURG

LORRAINE

FRANCHE
COMTÉ

SWISS
CANTONS

VALTELLINE

FRANCE

VENICE

BRESSE,
BUGEY,
GEX
(gained 1601)

SAVOY

MANTUA

DUCHY OF
MILAN

PARMA

TUSCANY

MODENA

SPAIN

PAPAL
STATES

• Rome

MEDITERRANEAN
SEA

⊢————⊣ 100 miles

◀━ ━ ━▶ The routes of the
'Spanish Road'

France's Eastern Border c. 1610

Road. Thus by the end of his reign, Henry had effectively turned the tables on Spain in Italy. Instead of the King of Spain being able to use northern Italy as part of the encirclement of France, the Spanish forces there were themselves hemmed in. Savoy, Switzerland, Venice, Tuscany and Rome surrounded the Spanish possessions in north Italy and Spanish communications northwards into the heart of Europe were threatened.

* Confrontation with Spain could not, however, be postponed indefinitely. In 1609 the Catholic Duke John William of Jülich-Cleves died. His possessions abutted the Netherlands and were thus of critical strategic importance to the Habsburgs. John William was childless and there were a number of claimants, Protestant and Catholic alike, to the inheritance. In order to prevent Jülich-Cleves falling into the hands of one of the Protestant German princes, Spanish troops from the Netherlands promptly occupied the duchy.

At this critical moment, the Jülich-Cleves crisis spilled over into French domestic politics. Henry IV had long lusted after the young Charlotte of Montmorency, whom we are told had first aroused the King's interest while dancing before him in the costume of a nymph. In order to keep Charlotte at court, Henry annulled her engagement to a dashing *galant* and married her off to the unattractive Prince Henry II of Condé. Condé, however, was insulted by the King's continued dalliance with his bride and, with Charlotte in tow, he absconded to the Spanish Netherlands. The prince's refusal to return his wife not only frustrated the King's passion, but represented a dangerously embarrassing example of insubordination amongst the aristocracy. Not to be outdone, Henry demanded that the Spanish rulers of the Netherlands send the prince back. When they refused, Henry announced his intention to invade Jülich-Cleves unless all Spanish forces were withdrawn from the duchy. Early in 1610 Henry forged a military partnership with the Protestant princes of the German Evangelical Union, the principal anti-Habsburg organisation in the Empire. By May he had mustered 50 000 French troops in readiness for a war with Spain.

Historians are divided as to whether Henry genuinely planned to make war or whether he was simply practising 'brinkmanship'. Henry's intentions can only be guessed at, for he died before the crisis could turn into a war. Certainly, the opinion of the King's foreign minister, Villeroy, was that Henry did not need to use force to obtain his objective, but only to show that he was ready to do so. As Villeroy put it only three weeks after Henry's assassination, 'If our good master were not dead, he would not have had to bother to cross the Seine. The keys of Jülich would have been brought to him.' Had such an event occurred, Spain's humiliation must have been so enormous as to have led within a short space to a retaliatory invasion of France. That Henry was now prepared to accept such an eventuality is the measure of his confidence both in France's revived strength and in his ability to outmatch his rival in the game of international power-politics.

6 Conclusion

Seen in the context of the first decades of the seventeenth century, Henry's reign appears less a turning-point than an interlude. Henry's assassination in 1610 inaugurated a fresh period of minority rule with a regency in the hands of Marie de Medici, another inexperienced Italian Queen Mother. During the reign of Henry's son and successor, Louis XIII (1610–43), the government of the kingdom became once more the prey of ambitious aristocratic leaders, led again by a Prince of Condé. Alternately in league with the Huguenots and with Spain, Henry II of Condé strove to achieve an undisputed influence over the royal council and to make good his claim as heir to the throne. Within ten years of Henry IV's death, the aristocracy were in arms against the crown and the Huguenots were in revolt. Richelieu's ministry (1624–42) temporarily relieved domestic tensions by directing the energies of nobles and Huguenots alike into the Thirty Years War against the Habsburgs. But with the conclusion of hostilities in 1648, the old animosities reappeared. Government was paralysed by the obstruction of the Paris *parlement*, the aristocracy moved into rebellion, and the streets of Paris were barricaded. Only Mazarin's shrewd manipulation of events, and the staggering incompetence of the aristocratic leadership, prevented the rebellion of the *Frondes* (1648–53) from ushering in a prolonged period of civil war.

With the benefit of hindsight we may conclude that the reappearance of civil strife in the decades after Henry's death was predictable. During his reign, Henry had not sufficiently reformed the state as to remove the potential for violent resistance to the crown. He had not broken the aristocracy, merely bought off its more troublesome leaders. In the Edict of Nantes, the religious question had been addressed, but not solved. Likewise, the government and administration of the realm had been overhauled, but not radically reconstructed. The powers of the *parlements* remained untrimmed, and provincial estates were still able to defy royal instructions. Thus the possibility of rebellion remained and would continue to do so until absolutist rule could be established in its full vigour.

Of course, Henry IV may be absolved from blame for failing to accomplish the work of his seventeenth-century successors. He had neither the opportunity nor the resources to impose the full panoply of absolutist monarchy. His achievement could only be a more modest one: to renew rather than to reform. There is thus little in the work of either Henry IV or Sully to suggest a major redirection of policy. Impetus was given instead to rebuilding the authority of the crown along the traditional lines of French monarchy. It may well be that by

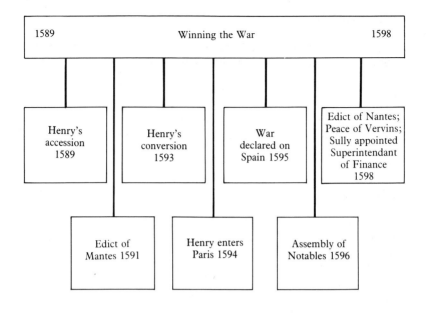

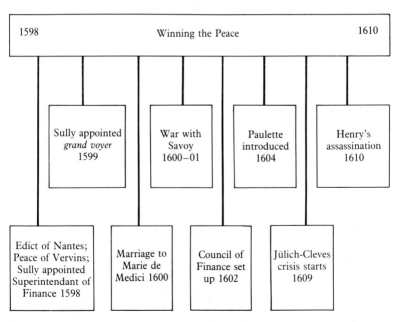

Summary of the Reign of Henry IV (1589–1610)

breathing new life into already-existing institutions, Henry revitalised government and made it capable of meeting the challenges of the seventeenth century. Such an analysis, however, ignores the work of Richelieu and Mazarin in maintaining royal authority during these tumultuous years. Henry's contribution must therefore be seen in narrower terms: as restoring to the crown what had been lost in the period of the civil wars. If by so reviving the prestige of kingship, Henry made possible the absolutism of Louis XIV, this was only because such a potential was already inherent in the very nature of sixteenth-century French monarchy.

Making notes on 'Henry IV'

This chapter is primarily concerned with assessing Henry IV's achievements and with establishing the limits of his success. The following questions and headings will help you make suitable notes:
1.   Introduction
2.   Religion
2.1. Relations with the Huguenots to 1598
2.2. The Edict of Nantes. What were the principal weaknesses from the Huguenot point-of-view of the Edict of Nantes?
3.   Finance and Administration
3.1. Financial problems and constraints
3.2. The work of Sully
3.3. The *paulette*
3.4. Towns, estates and *parlements*. How innovatory were the financial and administrative reforms undertaken by the Duke of Sully?
4.   Economy and Society
4.1. Recovery
4.2. Royal intervention and regulation
In what ways did the economic policies of Sully and Henry IV serve to strengthen the power of the crown?
5.   Foreign Policy
5.1. A Grand Design?
5.2. Limitations
5.3. War with Spain 1595–98
5.4. Foreign alliances
5.5. Jülich-Cleves. Why did Henry dispense with the cautious policies of the last ten years in response to the succession crisis in Jülich-Cleves?
6.   Conclusion. Is it fair to see Henry IV as a fundamentally conservative ruler? In what ways might his reign be considered innovatory?

Answering essay-questions on 'Henry IV'

A-level questions on the reign of Henry IV are usually straightforward and ask for an overall assessment of Henry's reign:

'What did Henry IV achieve as King of France?'

Occasionally, though, questions will approach Henry's achievements more indirectly:

'Have the achievements of Henry IV as King of France been exaggerated?'

'Do you agree that Henry IV's domestic and foreign policies were essentially conservative?'

Despite their different phrasing, each of the three questions requires you to give a full assessment of Henry's reign. It is rare for questions on Henry IV to concentrate exclusively on individual topics such as the work of the Duke of Sully or the Edict of Nantes.

In attempting the first question, do not confuse 'achieve' with 'do'. Construct a series of short sentences beginning, 'One of Henry's achievements was . . .', which may act as your plan. Rephrasing the question in such a way as to allow you to construct a series of sentences is a useful device for ensuring that what you write is relevant to the question being asked.

Candidates often fight shy of questions which seem to require a knowledge of historiography. In tackling the second question, do not feel you have to give an account of the views of various historians or to discuss the degree to which individual writers have exaggerated Henry's achievements. All you need to do is to indicate very broadly what the consensus of opinion is regarding the King: namely, that he restored the monarchy, revitalised the kingdom internally, and extended French influence abroad. Thereafter, you should explain each of these points more fully and indicate the limits of Henry's achievements. In your conclusion, you should explain clearly the extent to which you believe the prevailing impression of Henry IV to be correct.

Questions which begin with 'Do you agree that . . .' invite the division of your essay into two parts: the first recording the points where you agree with the opinion given, the second with areas of possible disagreement. On the whole, it is wise to write about equal amounts on each part. However, the evidence may appear to you to weigh so heavily in favour of one point of view that you devote most of your answer to explaining that part. If such is the case, let the reader know your opinion early on in the essay, preferably in your opening paragraph. Otherwise, it may be imagined that you do not know sufficient facts to give a balanced assessment. Although it may seem strange, A-level examiners are, like your teachers, actually on your side. They genuinely want to give high marks and to reward rather than to penalise. In writing your A-level answers, keep the examiner in the picture; make him aware of your viewpoint and of why you hold your opinions. Once the examiner understands your basic reasoning, he is more likely to follow and be sympathetic to your arguments.

Source-based questions on 'Henry IV'

1 Finance
Read the extracts given on pages 105 and 106 and answer the following questions:
a) What do the two extracts identify as the principal problems attending the financial administration of France during the 1590s?
b) How did Sully's methods, as outlined by him in the second extract, help to rebuild the kingdom's financial administration? What other methods did Sully use to restore the royal finances?
c) On the basis of what you have just read of Sully's memoirs, explain how reliable a source you think his autobiography is for the reign of Henry IV.

2 The Personal Authority of Henry IV
Read the extracts taken from the King's speeches on pages 104 and 109, and look at the picture of Henry IV given on page 101. Answer the following questions:
a) What arguments does Henry use to the townsmen of Toulouse to convince them that they ought to implement the Edict of Nantes?
b) What reasons does Henry give in the second extract for demanding the Paris *parlement*'s full obedience to his commands?
c) To what extent might the engraving of Henry IV have reinforced popular loyalty to the crown? Look in particular at the way Henry is presented in the picture and at the contents of the *cartouches* on the top right and left.

Further Reading

There are four short books, written with sixth-formers and students in mind, which can be recommended without hesitation:

R. J. Knecht, *French Renaissance Monarchy: Francis I and Henry II* (Longman: Seminar Studies in History, 1984)
Mark Greengrass, *The French Reformation* (Blackwell, 1987)
N. M. Sutherland, *Catherine de Medici and the Ancien Regime* (Historical Association pamphlet 1966, revised 1978)
Robin Briggs, *Early Modern France 1560–1715* (Oxford University Press, 1977), especially pages 1–34.

It may well be that you will wish to explore further some of the questions which this book and other short works only deal with briefly. In such a case, it would be worth looking at some of the books listed below, reading selectively by reference to chapter headings and index.

David Buisseret, *Henry IV* (George Allen and Unwin, 1984)
Mark Greengrass, *France in the Age of Henri IV: The Struggle for Stability* (Longman, 1984)
Mack P. Holt, *The Duke of Anjou and the Politique Struggle during the Wars of Religion* (Cambridge University Press, 1986)
R. J. Knecht, *Francis I* (Cambridge University Press, 1986)
J. E. Neale, *The Age of Catherine de Medici* (1943 and subsequent editions)
H. A. Lloyd, *The State, France and the Sixteenth Century* (George Allen and Unwin, 1983)
David Parker, *The Making of French Absolutism* (Edward Arnold, 1983)
J. H. M. Salmon, *Society in Crisis: France in the Sixteenth Century* (Benn, 1975)
Desmond Seward, *Prince of the Renaissance: The Life of Francis I* (Cardinal, 1974)
J. H. Shennan, *Government and Society in France 1461–1661* (George Allen and Unwin, 1969)
N. M. Sutherland, *The Massacre of St Bartholomew and the European Conflict* (Macmillan, 1973)
N. M. Sutherland, *The Huguenot Struggle for Recognition* (Yale University Press, 1980)
N. M. Sutherland, *Princes, Politics and Religion 1547–89* (Hambledon Press, 1984)

Sources on France: Renaissance Religion and Recovery, 1494–1610

Documentary appendices are provided in:

J. H. Shennan, *Government and Society in France 1461–1661* (George Allen and Unwin, 1969) pages 75–155.
R. J. Knecht, *French Renaissance Monarchy: Francis I and Henry II* (Longman: Seminar Studies in History, 1984) pages 78–103.
Philippe Erlanger, *St Bartholomew's Night* (Weidenfeld and Nicolson, 1962) pages 229–55.

For the Italian Wars, the following sources are available:

Francesco Guicciardini, *The History of Italy,* trans. Sidney Alexander (Macmillan, 1969)
Philippe de Commynes, *Memoirs* (2 vols), trans. S. Kinser (University of South Carolina Press, 1973)

Acknowledgements

The publishers would like to thank the following for their permission to reproduce copyright illustrations:

The Mansell Collection Limited, cover; Cliché des Musées Nationaux, Paris, page 18; Photographie Giraudon, pages 24, 46, 72, 80.

Every effort has been made to trace copyright holders of the following: pages 22 and 101.

Index